C000137163

3-Minute
POWER
PRAYERS
to
Start Your
Day

© 2023 by Barbour Publishing, Inc.

Print ISBN 978-1-63609-456-4

All rights reserved. No part of this publication may be reproduced or transmitted for commercial purposes, except for brief quotations in printed reviews, without written permission of the publisher. Reproduced text may not be used on the World Wide Web.

Churches and other noncommercial interests may reproduce portions of this book without the express written permission of Barbour Publishing, provided that the text does not exceed 500 words or 5 percent of the entire book, whichever is less, and that the text is not material quoted from another publisher. When reproducing text from this book, include the following credit line: "From *3-Minute Prayers to Start Your Day*, published by Barbour Publishing, Inc. Used by permission."

Scripture quotations marked ESV are from The Holy Bible, English Standard Version®, copyright © 2001 by Crossway Bibles, a publishing ministry of Good News Publishers. The ESV® text has been reproduced in cooperation with and by permission of Good News Publishers. Unauthorized reproduction of this publication is prohibited. All rights reserved.

Scripture quotations marked MSG are from *THE MESSAGE.* Copyright © by Eugene H. Peterson 1993, 1994, 1995, 1996, 2000, 2001, 2002. Used by permission of NavPress Publishing Group.

Scripture quotations marked NASB are taken from the New American Standard Bible © 1960, 1971, 1977, 1995, 2020 by The Lockman Foundation. All rights reserved.

Scripture quotations marked NIV are taken from the HOLY BIBLE, NEW INTERNATIONAL VERSION®. NIV®. Copyright © 1973, 1978, 1984, 2011 by Biblica, Inc.™ Used by permission. All rights reserved worldwide.

Published by Barbour Publishing, Inc., 1810 Barbour Drive, Uhrichsville, Ohio 44683, www.barbourbooks.com

Our mission is to inspire the world with the life-changing message of the Bible.

Printed in China.

RENAE BRUMBAUGH GREEN

3-Minute
POWER
PRAYERS
to
Start Your
Day

BARBOUR

PUBLISHING

Introduction

Quiet down before GOD, be prayerful before him.
PSALM 37:7 MSG

These encouraging prayers are especially for those days when you are weary from the busyness of everyday life and your soul is longing for a quiet time of refreshment in the heavenly Creator's calming presence. Three minutes from your hectic day is all you'll need to fill your cup to overflowing with strength for life's journey.

- Minute 1: Read and reflect on God's Word.

- Minute 2: Pray, using the provided prayer to jump-start a conversation with God.

- Minute 3: Reflect on a question for further thought.

Although this book isn't meant as a tool for deep Bible study, each soul-stirring prayer can be a touchstone to keep you grounded and focused on the one who hears all your prayers. May this book give you confidence in your status as God's child and remind you that your heavenly Father cares about everything you have to say. Go on. . .start your day by talking to Him. He's ready and waiting to hear from you!

Saturated

I will give thanks to the LORD with all my heart; I will tell of all Your wonders. I will rejoice and be jubilant in You; I will sing praise to Your name, O Most High.
PSALM 9:1-2 NASB

Dear Father, when I stop and consider all the wonderful things You've done for me, I'm overwhelmed with Your goodness. Sometimes I get distracted by negative events in my life, and I forget how amazing You are. I forget how much You love me. But all it takes is a moment, Father, of focused attention on all the ways You've blessed me, and I realize how You've saturated my life with good things. When people ask how I'm doing, give me boldness to tell them how great You are. I will keep a smile on my face and praise You today, Lord. Thank You for Your marvelous, mind-blowing love.

How has God surprised you with His blessings?

A New Song

God, I will sing a new song to You; on a harp
of ten strings I will sing praises to You.
PSALM 144:9 NASB

Dear Father, You're so gracious to give me a fresh start, every single day. Your love astonishes me, and I can't keep quiet. Though I can never repay Your goodness, I do want to offer my thanks. Today and every day, I will sing a new song to You. Whether out loud or in my heart, I want to praise You for Your overwhelming kindness to me. Whether on the harp, a piano keyboard, or a computer keyboard, I want every stroke, every action I complete to be an act of praise. Walk with me today, Lord. Fill my thoughts, guide my words, and direct my steps. May my life be a song that draws others to You and makes You smile.

How can you sing to God today
through your actions?

The Goodness of God

For You, Lord, are good, and ready to forgive,
and abundant in mercy to all who call upon You.
PSALM 86:5 NASB

Dear Father, this is such a beautiful description of Your character. Yet even these words don't begin to cover how good, how merciful, how kind, how amazing and awesome You are. Your goodness is beyond my comprehension, and yet You pour it out on me each day. When I mess up, You are quick to forgive me the moment I repent. I don't deserve Your love, and yet You lavish it freely on my life. I can't get away from Your goodness. . .You chase me down in order to bless me. Thank You for this overwhelming, abundant love. Today and every day, may my life reflect my humble thanks to You.

How has God poured out His love
to you? Dwell on His goodness today.

Give Thanks

Give thanks to the LORD, for He is good;
for His faithfulness is everlasting.
1 CHRONICLES 16:34 NASB

Give thanks. Two simple words, one syllable each. Yet when I set my mind on thanking You for all the wonderful things You've done, I'm overwhelmed. How can I possibly express my gratitude, with my limited vocabulary and my inadequate comprehension? Your blessings have saturated my life, spilling out onto the ground. I can't get away from Your goodness! Though I can never fully understand all the ways You've shown Your love to me, I'll try. Thank You for Jesus and the gift of salvation. Thank You for life and air and family and friends. Thank You for the beauty of Your creation. Today and every day, I will set my mind on Your goodness. With every breath, I want to thank You.

Have you ever tried to write God a thank-you note? Consider what you'd say to Him.

Praise God!

Praise the LORD! Oh give thanks to the LORD,
for He is good; for His mercy is everlasting.
PSALM 106:1 NASB

Dear Father, one dictionary defines *praise* as the act of expressing approval or admiration. I'm so limited in my ability to praise You as You deserve to be praised, but that won't keep me from trying. You are incomprehensible in Your goodness, indescribable in Your love. You are holy, perfect in every way. Yet despite Your majesty, You noticed me. You bent down, scooped me into Your arms, and whispered, *"You're Mine."* You discarded the filthy rags of my spirit, gave me a luxurious bubble bath in Your love, and clothed me in garments fit for royalty. The word *good* doesn't come close to describing You. With all that is in me, I praise You! You have my whole heart, for my whole life.

How has God shown His goodness to you today?

Surprising Love

Do not remember the sins of my youth or my wrongdoings; remember me according to Your faithfulness, for Your goodness' sake, LORD. The LORD is good and upright; therefore He instructs sinners in the way.

PSALM 25:7-8 NASB

Dear Father, when I think of Your love for me, it blows my mind. I'm undeserving. I've made many mistakes, and I've broken many of Your laws. But Your love—it catches me by surprise, and I almost lose my breath. When You look at me, You don't see my past. You don't see my mistakes or failures. You only see Your cherished child. Thank You for viewing me through the lens of Your love. I want my entire life to be a continuous act of gratitude. But I can't do that without Your guidance and instruction. Hold my hand today, Father. Show me how to be good like You.

Do you see yourself differently than God sees you? Describe the difference.

Waiting for Answers

Answer me, LORD, for Your mercy is good; according to the greatness of Your compassion, turn to me.
PSALM 69:16 NASB

Dear Father, You know every need of my heart. You feel every hurt and count every tear. You rejoice with my successes and support me through failures. That's why I know I can come to You with anything. Any struggle or temptation isn't a surprise to You, and You won't judge me for my weakness. Instead, You'll show mercy and compassion. You'll be pleased at my cries for help. You hear the secret pleas of my spirit. Please open my ears and sharpen my understanding as I listen for Your answers. Thank You for loving me tenderly and helping me through every trial. Today, I lay all my problems before You, and I'll wait with confidence for Your direction.

What do you need to hear from God about? Talk to Him, and wait for His answers.

The Gift of Peace

*"Glory to God in the highest, and on earth peace
among those with whom he is pleased!"*
LUKE 2:14 ESV

Dear Father, I've seen this verse countless times on Christmas cards. But just now, as I read it, I noticed the last part of it. This translation says, "Peace among those with whom he is pleased." Your promises are for those who please You, not for those who disrespect You and rebel against Your laws. When I lack peace in my life, maybe I should step back, examine my heart, and ask if You're pleased with me. When I'm right with You, I can have peace in the midst of even the worst circumstances. Your peace is a gift You've already given me, but it's a gift that works best when I'm close to You, when I'm living a life that pleases You.

*Do you feel that God is pleased with
you right now? Draw close to Him,
and take hold of His peace.*

Generous

And he answered them, "Whoever has two tunics is to share with him who has none, and whoever has food is to do likewise."
Luke 3:11 esv

Dear Father, You have been so generous with me. Not only did You give me the gift of salvation through Christ, but each day of my life You've poured out Your love on me. I have so many blessings, I can't begin to count them all. You made me in Your image, and my purpose is to become like You. Since You are generous with me, I should be generous with others. Forgive me for being stingy with my resources and my good opinions. Forgive me for holding back, thinking others are less worthy than I am. Teach me to be generous, whether I'm giving financial support or simply a smile and a kind word.

How is God calling you to be generous today?

A Place to Belong

For those whom he foreknew he also predestined to be conformed to the image of his Son, in order that he might be the firstborn among many brothers.

ROMANS 8:29 ESV

Dear Father, much of the time I feel lost in this world. I feel lonely even in a crowd, like I don't fit in. I don't know my place here. But this verse reminds me that Jesus is my Brother. He's the firstborn, and I'm His younger sibling. No matter what happens, I'm "in." I belong. I feel out of place in this world because it's not my home, but I know there's a place where I fit: in Your home. I've been grafted into Your lineage. I'm part of the dynasty, with the full inheritance of a beloved child. Thank You for giving me a place to belong.

Do you struggle to fit in? You fit perfectly within God's family. You're His child!

Faith Building

*So faith comes from hearing, and hearing
through the word of Christ.*
ROMANS 10:17 ESV

Dear Father, I want to be a person of great faith. In my head, I know the promises. I know about Your power and love and greatness. I know nothing is impossible with You. But acting out that faith is a little harder. When giants loom, when stressful circumstances swirl around me, I turn into a puddle of fear and anxiety. I forget all about how big You are as I focus on how big the problem is. The answer to my lack of faith is to burrow deep in Your Word. As I fill my mind with Your wisdom, it becomes part of me. It shows up in the midst of the storm and pulls my attention back to You. Help me make Your Word a part of my daily routine, as I work to build my faith.

How much time do you spend daily in God's Word? Can you increase that by 10 percent?

What to Wear

*But put on the Lord Jesus Christ, and make no
provision for the flesh, to gratify its desires.*

ROMANS 13:14 ESV

Dear Father, each morning, when I get dressed for the
day, I consider what I'll wear. I try to look nice and clean
and appropriate for that day's activities. Too often, I don't
consider what I'll wear, or "put on," spiritually. I roll out
of bed, and whatever outlook claims me is the one I keep
for the day. Whether anxiety or despair or a grumbly
attitude, that's what I wear. Help me put on Christ, as
this verse says. Each day when others look at me, I want
them to see a person clothed in Your righteousness.
When I interact with the world, I want to do so as one
wearing Christ's royal robe. Help me put on His garments
of humility, kindness, and love.

*How do you decide what clothes you'll wear each
day? Spend time preparing your spirit as well.*

Everlasting Goodness

*For the LORD is good; His mercy is everlasting
and His faithfulness is to all generations.*
PSALM 100:5 NASB

Dear Father, this verse reminds me of the old commercial about the Energizer Bunny. Your mercy keeps going and going and going. Your faithfulness stretches into eternity. Your goodness travels deeper and higher and wider than my limited mind can fathom. Today, as I face problems and trials with work, family, relationships, or anything else, remind me of Your goodness. Keep me from worry and stress as I sink into Your overwhelming love for me. My confidence is in You alone, and Your grace is more than enough to see me through any situation. Make me a reflection of Your love to those around me. I love You completely, and I trust You with my whole heart.

*How does God's goodness in the past
give you confidence in the future?*

Nothing Is Impossible

"For nothing will be impossible with God."
LUKE 1:37 ESV

Dear Father, this one short sentence, spoken by the angel to Mary, holds such power. I don't know why I think some things are possible and others aren't. Nothing is too hard for You. You created the universe. You allowed a young peasant girl, a virgin, to give birth to Your Son. You can do anything! When worries, fears, and concerns pass through my mind today, remind me of this verse. My loved one who doesn't know You? I'll pray, believing that nothing is impossible with You. That financial hardship? I'll trust You because You can do anything. Whatever mountain stands in my way, I'll just tell it to move, in Your name. I praise You, Father, because nothing is too difficult for You.

What problem in your life seems impossible?
Give it to God and let Him handle it.

God's Servant

*And Mary said, "Behold, I am the servant of
the Lord; let it be to me according to your
word." And the angel departed from her.*
LUKE 1:38 ESV

Dear Father, what a beautiful soul Mary must have
been for You to choose her as the mother of Your Son.
This passage shows her faith and her willingness to
do whatever You asked. Do I have that kind of heart?
I want to. Sometimes it feels like the things You ask of
me are too hard. Maybe they're inconvenient, or I don't
feel qualified. Too often, my first response is to give You
reasons why I can't obey You. But like Mary, I want to
please You. I am Your servant, Lord. I will do whatever
You want, according to Your plan for my life.

*Has God called you to do something
difficult? Answer Him as Mary did: "I am
Your servant. I'll do whatever You ask."*

Humble and Strong

*We who are strong ought to bear with the
failings of the weak and not to please ourselves.
Each of us should please our neighbors for their
good, to build them up. For even Christ did not
please himself but, as it is written: "The insults
of those who insult you have fallen on me."*

ROMANS 15:1–3 NIV

Dear Father, this scripture is the opposite of the worldly
point of view that says to please yourself. It goes
against human nature to be humble and put others first.
But that's what You've called me to do. Putting myself
first indicates that I'm weak and immature. The world
sees humility as weakness, like a doormat, but You see
it as strength. Indeed, it takes strength of character to
set aside my own desires in favor of someone else's.
Make me humble and strong, like You.

*In what situation do you
find it hard to be humble?*

Tell Your Story

And I, when I came to you, brothers, did not come proclaiming to you the testimony of God with lofty speech or wisdom. For I decided to know nothing among you except Jesus Christ and him crucified.

1 CORINTHIANS 2:1-2 ESV

Dear Father, sometimes I worry about how to share my faith. I don't feel qualified, or I worry that I'll say the wrong thing. But anyone can share how great You are! I don't need fancy words or a seminary degree. All I need to do is tell my story about all the amazing things You've done in my life. Forgive me for being self-conscious. Make me bold to tell others about You. I know people are parched for the living water only You can give, and I have the ability to show them the well.

What people has God placed in your life so you can share His love with them? Just tell your story.

Streams of Water

"For the LORD your God is bringing you into a good land, a land of streams of water, of fountains and springs, flowing out in valleys and hills."
DEUTERONOMY 8:7 NASB

Dear Father, You made this promise of blessing to Your people, Israel. But I claim this promise for my life as well because I am Yours. I belong to You. I know that as You lead me into a good place, I may have to wander in the desert for a while. But I have confidence in Your goodness. I know You love me, and Your plans for me are better than I can hope or imagine. Wherever You lead, I will hold tight to Your hand. Whatever I must endure, I will trust You, knowing You're bringing me to a good land that's filled with life-giving water, with fountains and springs of Your mercy, flowing into the valleys and hills of my life.

Do you feel that you're wandering in the desert? Trust His goodness.

Never Doubt

And Zechariah said to the angel, "How shall I know this? For I am an old man, and my wife is advanced in years." And the angel answered him, "I am Gabriel. I stand in the presence of God, and I was sent to speak to you and to bring you this good news. And behold, you will be silent and unable to speak until the day that these things take place, because you did not believe my words, which will be fulfilled in their time."

LUKE 1:18–20 ESV

Dear Father, to some this may seem rather harsh. But Zechariah had served You for many years. His faith should have been stronger. When we're at a place in our lives where we should trust You but instead we doubt You, there are consequences. Am I mature in my faith, Lord? I don't want to question You. You have never ever failed me. I have no reason to doubt.

Have you questioned God when you should have trusted?

By Faith

For I am not ashamed of the gospel, for it is the power of God for salvation to everyone who believes, to the Jew first and also to the Greek. For in it the righteousness of God is revealed from faith for faith, as it is written, "The righteous shall live by faith."

ROMANS 1:16–17 ESV

Dear Father, Your gospel is what allows each of us to have a relationship with You. Because of the good news of salvation through Your Son, Jesus Christ, I can be righteous, or in right standing with You. The last part of this passage says, "The righteous shall live by faith." Do I live by faith? Or do I just say I have faith but live however I please? Do I really believe all the things I say I believe? I want to. Teach me to let my actions match my words. Help me live by faith.

Are there areas where you lack faith? Ask God to increase your faith in Him.

Don't Judge

Therefore you have no excuse, O man, every one of you who judges. For in passing judgment on another you condemn yourself, because you, the judge, practice the very same things.

ROMANS 2:1 ESV

Dear Father, I don't know why it's so easy for me to pass judgment on other people. I do it all the time, though I don't want to. On the surface I try to show compassion and kindness and understanding. But deep down I compare myself to others. And when I think I've come out ahead, I'm secretly pleased. Forgive me! I am in no place to judge any other person. Only You have that right, and You are a gracious, kind Judge to all who are truly sorry, who want to please You. Give me humility, and guard my thoughts from judging others.

Is there someone you've secretly judged? Pray for that person instead, and rejoice over their successes.

Be a Doer

*For it is not the hearers of the law who
are righteous before God, but the doers
of the law who will be justified.*
ROMANS 2:13 ESV

Dear Father, I've heard Your Word all my life. In many ways, the Bible is part of our culture. But hearing the Bible doesn't help me become like You any more than listening to the radio will teach me to play the piano. If I want to become righteous, I must make Your words a part of me. I do this by acting out Your commands. I do this by loving people, acting justly, showing kindness and compassion, and practicing humility before You and others. Each time I hear Your Word, let it soak into the roots of my soul. I want my life to be a living, breathing testament to who You are.

*In what ways can you adjust your
actions to match God's Word?*

God's Promises

"Now behold, today I am going the way of all the earth, and you know in all your hearts and in all your souls that not one word of all the good words which the LORD your God spoke concerning you has failed; they all have been fulfilled for you, not one of them has failed."

JOSHUA 23:14 NASB

Dear Father, You've made so many life-giving promises in Your Word. Every single one of them is true, and You always keep Your Word. But many of those promises are made to those who love You, who follow You with all their heart. I can't make use of those promises in my life if I don't know what they are. Help me spend time in Your Word, becoming familiar with Your promises. I want to know You, Lord. I want to spend time with You and listen to what You have to say. When I get distracted, pull me back to You.

What is your favorite promise that God made to you?

Statement of Purpose

"But I do not account my life of any value nor as precious to myself, if only I may finish my course and the ministry that I received from the Lord Jesus, to testify to the gospel of the grace of God."

ACTS 20:24 ESV

Dear Father, my life is not my own. It is Yours to do with as You please. I know my comfort and rest will come when my work here is done. Any comfort I receive while I'm here is just a bonus, given to me because of Your great love. Yet those pleasures are not to guide my purpose in this life. This is a hard prayer to say, Lord, and yet here I am, meaning every word. I'm Yours. I belong to You. Do with me what You will.

What is your main goal or purpose in life? How does that align with God's plan for you?

In Spite of Failure

"But go, tell his disciples and Peter that he is going before you to Galilee. There you will see him, just as he told you."

MARK 16:7 ESV

Dear Father, at this point, I know Peter was embarrassed and ashamed. After promising he'd never deny Christ, he did so three times. His shame caused him to separate from the other disciples. But You took our shame! You are the lifter of our heads (Psalm 3:3). Thank You for this reminder that I should never let shame over past mistakes keep me from fellowship with other believers or from serving You. We've all messed up. You show grace and mercy. You care more about what I'm going to do than what I've done. And like the man in the parable of the lost sheep, You'll leave the ninety-nine to come after me when I go astray. Thank You for loving me and wanting me in spite of my failures.

Are you ashamed of something in your past? Let God lift your head. He loves you.

Like an Angel

And gazing at him, all who sat in the council
saw that his face was like the face of an angel.
ACTS 6:15 ESV

Dear Father, in this passage, they were gazing at Stephen, who was about to be stoned for his belief in Christ. He was facing death for his faith, and yet his face held a serenity that reminded them of an angel. When others look at me, what do they see? Too often, they see frustration or worry or fear or distractedness. But I want them to see You. When people look at me, I want them to see Your glory, Your power, and Your grace. I want Your presence to be so strong in my life that others can see a physical difference in my countenance. Our facial expressions are often a window to our hearts. When people look at me, I want them to see You.

What messages do your facial
expressions send to others?

For Good

And Saul approved of his execution. And there arose on that day a great persecution against the church in Jerusalem, and they were all scattered throughout the regions of Judea and Samaria, except the apostles.

ACTS 8:1 ESV

Dear Father, Saul (later Paul) could have carried this shame with him for the rest of his life. It could have been a debilitating shame—he approved of Stephen's execution, and of many others as well. Yet You have a way of causing all things to work together for good for those who love You, who are called according to Your purpose (Romans 8:28). This wretched persecution caused believers to scatter. As they scattered, they carried Your good news with them, to the far reaches of the earth. Paul went on to write much of the New Testament. Thank You for this reminder that You can turn even the worst circumstances around for good.

What circumstance in your life seems beyond redemption? Let go and leave it with God. He will turn it around.

His Words Are Truth

"Now then, Lord GOD, You are God, and Your
words are truth; and You have promised
this good thing to Your servant."

2 SAMUEL 7:28 NASB

Dear Father, Your promises aren't the same as a promise given by another person. With You, saying something and doing it are not two separate acts. Once You say something, it is final. You have promised me peace. You've promised me joy. You've promised to supply all my needs, and You've promised never to leave me or turn Your back on me. Thank You for the truth, the finality of Your words. Forgive me for ever doubting Your goodness and for treating Your promises like they're not a sure thing. When circumstances cause me to worry, remind me of these vows, and help me rest with confidence in Your Word.

What promise has God made to you that
you struggle to believe when times are hard?
Be confident in the finality of His Word.

Fresh Start

*"Blessed are those whose lawless deeds are forgiven,
and whose sins are covered; blessed is the man
against whom the Lord will not count his sin."*
ROMANS 4:7–8 ESV

Dear Father, these verses are talking about me! I have messed up so many times, in so many ways. But I'm blessed because You don't hold those blunders or rebellions against me. The moment I realize my mistake and want to change, You wipe my mistake away. You are the God of fresh starts. Thank You for giving me so many second chances, Lord. Teach me to show the same kind of love to others. Give me wisdom for how to react when others fail me. Show me what it means to truly forgive. I want to extend second chances to others when appropriate. Make me a beacon of Your grace.

*Is there a person in your life
who has wronged you? Ask God
to help you forgive and move on.*

About Faith

*No unbelief made him waver concerning the
promise of God, but he grew strong in his faith as
he gave glory to God, fully convinced that God
was able to do what he had promised. That is why
his faith was "counted to him as righteousness."*
ROMANS 4:20-22 ESV

Dear Father, this verse is about Abraham. He had every
reason to be anxious. You told him to take his wife and
go, but You didn't tell him where he was going. You told
him his descendants would outnumber the stars, yet
You didn't give him a son until he was far too old, by
human standards, to father children. You promised, and
Abraham lived in faith. You've promised good things to
me as well. Forgive me for not trusting Your goodness.
Help me live in hope, with the faith of Abraham.

*In what situation do you struggle to believe
God? Does anxiety and doubt keep you
from operating in confidence and faith?*

Chain of Events

*Not only that, but we rejoice in our sufferings,
knowing that suffering produces endurance, and
endurance produces character, and character
produces hope, and hope does not put us to shame,
because God's love has been poured into our hearts
through the Holy Spirit who has been given to us.*
ROMANS 5:3-5 ESV

Dear Father, how can I rejoice in my sufferings? That seems counterintuitive to everything in my human nature. Yet if I follow the chain of consequences in this scripture, I see that eventually suffering leads to hope, or confidence in the good things You've promised. I can have hope because of Your love. You pour it out on me. I breathe it in, until there's no more room for fear. Whatever hardships I face, I will face them with confidence, knowing I operate on a different kind of fuel—the fuel of Your grace and goodness in my life. Thank You for the good things I know are coming.

*How has suffering developed endurance
and character in your life?*

Life and Peace

For to set the mind on the flesh is death, but to set the mind on the Spirit is life and peace.

ROMANS 8:6 ESV

Dear Father, why is it so easy to understand something in my head but so hard to put it into practice? Most of the things I worry about are just temporary things. Most of the circumstances that tug my anxiety into high speed are earthly, flesh-and-blood problems. When I center my thoughts on this world, I get stressed out, and my quality of life plummets. But when I keep my eyes on You, when I focus my mind on eternity, I have peace in the midst of even the worst situations. Remind me to set my mind on Your Spirit today. I look forward to the life and peace that will follow.

What does your mind automatically turn to when you're not focusing? You can retrain your thoughts to turn to Christ.

Rest

"Blessed be the LORD, who has given rest to His people Israel in accordance with everything that He promised; not one word has failed of all His good promise, which He promised through Moses His servant."

1 KINGS 8:56 NASB

Dear Father, You gave rest to Your people. What a beautiful gift. As Your child, I want to ask for the same gift today. I need rest. I'm tired, Lord, and though I try to relax, though I try to sleep, my mind races with worry. I know that's a sign that I'm not trusting You with my problems. Today, I claim Your promise of rest. Calm my mind. Give me peace and serenity. Put a smile on my face and joy in my heart. In the midst of my work and my busyness, help my spirit rest in You. Thank You for all Your good promises.

Do you feel rested? Trust Him with all the things that rob you of your peace.

Rolled Back

And they were saying to one another, "Who will roll away the stone for us from the entrance of the tomb?" And looking up, they saw that the stone had been rolled back—it was very large.

MARK 16:3-4 ESV

Dear Father, how many times do I worry about a problem, only to find You've already taken care of it? When You said to be anxious for nothing, You weren't kidding. You see me, every moment of my life. Not a thing happens to me that You don't already know about in advance. And when boulders stand in the way of what You have planned for me, You've already made arrangements to roll those stones away. I don't have to stress and scheme and figure things out for myself. All I have to do is follow You, trust Your plan, and watch You work miracles in my life.

What problem seems like a boulder to you right now? Trust God to roll it away.

Intimate

For who knows a person's thoughts except their own spirit within them? In the same way no one knows the thoughts of God except the Spirit of God. What we have received is not the spirit of the world, but the Spirit who is from God, so that we may understand what God has freely given us. This is what we speak, not in words taught us by human wisdom but in words taught by the Spirit, explaining spiritual realities with Spirit-taught words.

1 CORINTHIANS 2:11–13 NIV

Dear Father, to know a person's spirit is to know them intimately. You didn't just leave me with a bunch of rules and descriptions. You sent Your Holy Spirit to pursue me and to know me, so I can truly know You. I want to know You deeply, personally. Thank You for the gentle, genuine familiarity that comes with truly belonging to You.

Do you want to know God more? Ask His Holy Spirit to reveal Himself to you.

The Prize

*Do you not know that in a race all the runners
run, but only one gets the prize? Run in such a
way as to get the prize. Everyone who competes
in the games goes into strict training. They
do it to get a crown that will not last, but we
do it to get a crown that will last forever.*

1 CORINTHIANS 9:24-25 NIV

Dear Father, thank You for this reminder that I need to keep my eye on the prize. Though I won't receive the true prize on this side of eternity, I know the prize is real. It isn't like the awards and accolades I receive here on earth. Those provide only a temporary thrill. This life is short, and earthly trophies will end up in a trash heap, abandoned and forgotten. I want the eternal prize, Father. Help me focus on eternity.

*What are your goals for this life?
Will they last for eternity?*

The Flower

What you sow does not come to life unless it dies.
When you sow, you do not plant the body that will
be, but just a seed, perhaps of wheat or of something
else. But God gives it a body as he has determined,
and to each kind of seed he gives its own body.
1 CORINTHIANS 15:36–38 NIV

Dear Father, a seed must die for something glorious to come. When I plant flower seeds in my garden, those seeds eventually burst open and a beautiful plant emerges. The seed is just a husk, left to disintegrate in the soil. I understand that this body of mine is merely the seed, the husk, for eternity. Thank You for watering and nurturing my spirit in preparation for the new life to come. Help me stay focused on the true flower of my life—my spirit—as I become exactly who You created me to be.

Has your focus been more on the seed
(earthly life) or the flower (eternity)?

Restore My Soul

The Law of the Lord is perfect,
restoring the soul; the testimony of
the Lord is sure, making wise the simple.
PSALM 19:7 NASB

Dear Father, to restore something means to repair it, to return it to its previous condition. It can also refer to returning something to a state of health, soundness, and vigor. My soul needs restoration. I long to be returned to the way You created us to be before sin entered the world. Your Word does that. It makes me more like Christ, more like You intended me to be in the first place. Your Word makes me wise with Your kind of wisdom, the kind that surpasses human understanding. I want to spend time in Your Word, today and every day. Restore my soul and make me wise.

In what way does your soul need to be restored? God's Word restores the soul.

A Cheerful Giver

Remember this: Whoever sows sparingly will also reap sparingly, and whoever sows generously will also reap generously. Each of you should give what you have decided in your heart to give, not reluctantly or under compulsion, for God loves a cheerful giver.

2 CORINTHIANS 9:6-7 NIV

Dear Father, You have given so freely to me. If I were to write out all my blessings, I couldn't find enough volumes to contain them. Your generosity takes my breath away. Teach me to find more joy in giving to others than in receiving for myself. Forgive me for hoarding things, whether it's possessions, money, or something else. Forgive me for sowing sparingly. Show me where You want me to give my time, resources, or affection, and help me lavish it freely, even to those who haven't been generous with me. I want to love extravagantly, just as You love.

In what ways can you show generosity today?

Bragging Rights

But, "Let the one who boasts boast in the Lord."
For it is not the one who commends himself who is
approved, but the one whom the Lord commends.
2 CORINTHIANS 10:17–18 NIV

Dear Father, deep down, I want to impress people. I want them to think well of me. Too many of my actions are driven by wanting bragging rights. But that's so silly of me. Everything I have is because of You. Any gift or talent I have originated with You. Forgive me for being self-focused and for wanting to take the credit for anything good. I want to be humble, Father, except when it comes to You. If I boast about anything, let it be in how amazing, how wonderful, and how powerful You are. If I boast in anything, let it be in Your love. You alone deserve the praise for every good thing.

In what ways can you brag on God today?

Blessable

"Be careful to obey all these words that I command
you, that it may go well with you and with your
children after you forever, when you do what is good
and right in the sight of the LORD your God."
DEUTERONOMY 12:28 ESV

Dear Father, I want Your blessings. Every day, it seems I'm asking You for something else. But sometimes I forget that You gave me principles in Your Word to make me more "blessable." Your commands are in place for a reason: to help me live the best life possible. Those statutes keep me close to You and guard me against sin's destruction. When my children and others in my life see me living in a way that pleases You, it gives them a role model, and it makes it easier for them to live for You too. Help me, today and every day, to do what is good and right in Your sight.

In what way can you become more blessable?

Trust and Obey

"Go into the village in front of you, and immediately as you enter it you will find a colt tied, on which no one has ever sat. Untie it and bring it."

MARK 11:2 ESV

Dear Father, normally, an unbroken colt would need to be trained. It would initially have trouble with a rider. This colt didn't need to be trained, because animals obey their masters. You created this colt, and it submitted to Your Son. It wasn't even skittish with all the crowds, all the people shouting and waving and throwing things. Sometimes, You ask me to do things that don't make sense to me. Sometimes, You call me to do things I don't feel prepared for. I feel anxious and skittish because I don't know what will happen. Remind me to be like this colt. All I need to do is submit, obey, and trust You.

In what situation do you feel unprepared? Trust God. Obey His call, and let Him take care of the rest.

Transformed

And do not be conformed to this world, but be
transformed by the renewing of your mind,
so that you may prove what the will of God is,
that which is good and acceptable and perfect.
ROMANS 12:2 NASB

Dear Father, when I read this verse, I can't help but compare the two words *conform* and *transform*. A form is the shape or appearance of something. To conform means to comply, or to take on the shape of those around you. To transform means to change shape completely. You don't want me to comply with the standards of this world. Instead, You want to change me, to make me more like You. Forgive me for wanting to fit into this world, when that's not what You created me to do. Your goal is to make me good and holy and Christlike. Transform me into Your image, Father.

In what ways have you conformed to this world?
How does God want to transform your life?

Letter of Recommendation

You yourselves are our letter, written on our hearts, known and read by everyone. You show that you are a letter from Christ, the result of our ministry, written not with ink but with the Spirit of the living God, not on tablets of stone but on tablets of human hearts.

2 CORINTHIANS 3:2–3 NIV

Dear Father, what a high compliment! To say that someone's life is Your letter of recommendation is perhaps the highest honor that can be paid to one of Your followers. As I read this, I wonder if the same can be said of my own life. I want to live for You. I want every breath, every thought, every word, every action to make You proud and to reflect how amazing You are. Make me a letter of recommendation, open and laid bare for all to see Your goodness, mercy, and love.

When others look at your life, do they see God's goodness? Ask Him to make it so.

Promise Keeper

For no matter how many promises God has made, they are "Yes" in Christ. And so through him the "Amen" is spoken by us to the glory of God. Now it is God who makes both us and you stand firm in Christ. He anointed us, set his seal of ownership on us, and put his Spirit in our hearts as a deposit, guaranteeing what is to come.
2 CORINTHIANS 1:20–22 NIV

Dear Father, sometimes when I make a promise, I can't deliver on it. It's never on purpose. But even when I have the best of intentions, circumstances can prevent me from following through. That never happens with You. When You promise something, You always, always follow through. I can claim Your promises at any time, and You will deliver. I can only claim the promises I know about, though. Help me study Your Word and become familiar with Your promises so I can live the abundant life You want me to live.

Which of God's promises do you claim for yourself today?

Finding Worth

Such confidence we have through Christ before God. Not that we are competent in ourselves to claim anything for ourselves, but our competence comes from God. He has made us competent as ministers of a new covenant—not of the letter but of the Spirit; for the letter kills, but the Spirit gives life.

2 CORINTHIANS 3:4-6 NIV

Dear Father, I often feel like I don't measure up, like I'm not good enough to do Your work. But that's legalism, or "the letter of the law." You knew no one could be good enough without Christ. That's why You sent Him. My competence comes through You, through Your Spirit's work in my life, and not from anything I have or haven't done. My competence doesn't depend on me at all. . .it's all You. Thank You for making me new—and for making me like You.

In what ways do you feel that you don't measure up? Find your worth in Christ.

Set Apart

Therefore, "Come out from them and be separate, says the Lord. Touch no unclean thing, and I will receive you." And, "I will be a Father to you, and you will be my sons and daughters, says the Lord Almighty."

2 CORINTHIANS 6:17–18 NIV

Dear Father, thank You for this promise to be a Father to me, to adopt me and make me fully part of Your family. I am grateful beyond words. Help me honor the first part of this promise, to be separate from the world. As Your daughter, I am not supposed to entrench myself in worldliness. It's hard sometimes, living here but not really fitting in. But I know I fit in perfectly within Your family, and You are preparing my place even now. Help me to be set apart and to live in a way that honors You.

In what ways do you struggle to be set apart from the world?

Taste and See

*Taste and see that the LORD
is good; how blessed is the
man who takes refuge in Him!*
PSALM 34:8 NASB

Dear Father, this verse always reminds me of Thanksgiving, when the table is laden with the most delicious food imaginable and everyone gathers around to thank You for Your goodness. I often overeat on that particular holiday because every dish is mouthwatering and delectable. But I don't have to wait for Thanksgiving. You offer a banquet each time I read the Bible! Each morning, I can taste Your goodness. Why would I ever start my day with a sloppy spiritual meal when You've provided such an amazing pantry in Your Word? Today and every day, I want to feast in Your grace. I want to take refuge in Your love and satiate myself with Your presence. Thank You for Your bountiful blessings in my life.

*In what ways has God shown
His goodness in your life?*

Childlike

And they were bringing children to him that he might touch them, and the disciples rebuked them. But when Jesus saw it, he was indignant and said to them, "Let the children come to me; do not hinder them, for to such belongs the kingdom of God. Truly, I say to you, whoever does not receive the kingdom of God like a child shall not enter it." And he took them in his arms and blessed them, laying his hands on them.

MARK 10:13–16 ESV

Dear Father, I can see this scene in my mind like it's playing out on a movie screen. I picture these little children, so innocent, so trusting. Just as small children completely trust their parents to meet all their needs, You want me to trust You completely. When did I lose that trust, that innocence? Help me regain it, Father, as I trust You with my whole heart.

In what area do you struggle to trust God completely? Ask Him to help you regain a childlike faith.

See and Love

And Jesus, looking at him, loved him, and said to him, "You lack one thing: go, sell all that you have and give to the poor, and you will have treasure in heaven; and come, follow me."

MARK 10:21 ESV

Dear Father, these words, spoken by Jesus to the rich young ruler, are challenging. But perhaps an equal challenge is the attitude they were spoken with. As Christ looked at the man, He *loved* him. He didn't judge him. He didn't take his measure and find him lacking. Jesus spoke with sincerity of heart, wanting only the best for this young man. When I look at others, do I love them? Do I truly see people who desperately need You? Forgive me for failing to view others as You do. Give me Your heart, Father. Help me truly see, and truly love, those You place in my path.

Who does God want you to see and love today?

Because of Love

And taking the twelve again, he began to tell them what was to happen to him, saying, "See, we are going up to Jerusalem, and the Son of Man will be delivered over to the chief priests and the scribes, and they will condemn him to death and deliver him over to the Gentiles. And they will mock him and spit on him, and flog him and kill him. And after three days he will rise."
MARK 10:32-34 ESV

Dear Father, I'm sure it's Your mercy that prevents me from knowing the future. If I knew what was going to happen, I might avoid the very things You intend for my good, to shape me and make me like You. But Jesus knew exactly what was coming. He knew how wretched it would be. Still, He chose to proceed—because of love. Thank You for the love that endured unspeakable pain and torment so I wouldn't have to.

Can you measure the depth of God's love for you? Try anyway.

Have Faith

And Jesus said to him, "What do you want me to do for you?" And the blind man said to him, "Rabbi, let me recover my sight." And Jesus said to him, "Go your way; your faith has made you well." And immediately he recovered his sight and followed him on the way.

MARK 10:51-52 ESV

Dear Father, time and again in Your Word You commend faith. This man's sight was restored because of his faith. When we believe You will do something, You reward that faith. You may not always act in the way I want You to, but my pure, innocent confidence in Your love and power pleases You, and You've promised to honor that kind of reliance on You. I believe You are God. I believe in Your ultimate power and Your overwhelming love. Give me the faith of this blind man. I believe.

For what miracle are you waiting for today? Nothing is impossible with God. Have faith.

Stronghold

The LORD is good, a stronghold in the day of trouble, and He knows those who take refuge in Him.
NAHUM 1:7 NASB

Dear Father, why do I so easily forget these simple truths? You are good, and all Your actions are born of that goodness. You are my stronghold. When storms whip against my life, I can hold on to You, and I know You're holding on to me. I am Yours, and You will never let me go. Thank You for these reassuring promises. As I go about my day today, no matter what comes, I will rest in Your unfailing love. I will be confident in Your strength, knowing You protect me from every side. And to the best of my ability, I will point others to Your goodness and love.

How has God been your stronghold in troubled times? His love is fierce, and it will never let you down.

Love

*"'And you shall love the Lord your God with all
your heart and with all your soul and with all your
mind and with all your strength.' The second is this:
'You shall love your neighbor as yourself.' There
is no other commandment greater than these."*

MARK 12:30–31 ESV

Dear Father, love is at the heart of Your greatest
commandments. Not achievement or success, not
legalism or perfection. . .only love. I am to love You
with all that is in me. I am to love others and look
out for their wants and needs the way I look out for
myself. I also notice that You expect us to love ourselves.
That's important to You; You just don't want us putting
ourselves before others. I'm not sure how I measure up
to these commands. I admit, apart from You, I'm not
capable of such love. Teach me to love like You love.

*What aspect of loving God or others do you
struggle with most? Ask God to teach you.*

Rejected

Then Achish called David and said to him,
"As the LORD lives, you have been honest, and to
me it seems right that you should march out and in
with me in the campaign. For I have found nothing
wrong in you from the day of your coming to me to
this day. Nevertheless, the lords do not approve of
you. So go back now; and go peaceably, that you
may not displease the lords of the Philistines."
1 SAMUEL 29:6-7 ESV

Dear Father, David had done nothing wrong. Still he was pursued by Saul. He fled to Achish and lived honorably among the Philistines, but they rejected him too. David questioned Achish, but he didn't argue. He did as requested and left. As I live honorably for You, I still suffer rejection. Though I may not understand why, help me trust You to open doors for me as You see fit. Help me not to force myself in where I'm not wanted.

Have you felt rejected despite doing your best?

On Watch

*"Watch therefore, for you know
neither the day nor the hour."*
MATTHEW 25:13 ESV

Dear Father, I know You said we won't know the day or hour when You'll come back for us. But You did give us signs to watch for, and it sure seems like You're coming soon. Help me live each day, each hour, each moment as if it could be my last chance to please You. Pour out Your love and Your light through my life. With everyone I meet, let me be a beacon of Your kindness, compassion, and generosity. I know it's love that draws others to You, so help me love like You do, with reckless abandon. I want to be ready, with no regrets, on the day You arrive to take Your people home.

*If you knew Christ would return tomorrow, would
you make any changes to your life today?*

Alone

Then all the disciples left him and fled.
MATTHEW 26:56 ESV

Dear Father, You know what it feels like to be alone, don't You? I'm so sorry Jesus had to face the most difficult moment of His life without His friends by His side. How rejected He must have felt! Yet He moved forward with courage and conviction to fulfill His destiny. I often feel alone and rejected too. I feel like I don't fit in anywhere, and I long for loyal friends and deep connections. Help me be the kind of friend I want others to be to me: loyal, kind, and compassionate. And when I feel alone and rejected, help me press on, as Jesus did, with courage and conviction to live out Your purpose and plan for my life.

Have you ever felt rejected and alone? Does knowing Christ's situation help you feel less alone?

His Goodness

And He said, "I Myself will make all My goodness
pass before you, and will proclaim the name
of the LORD before you; and I will be gracious
to whom I will be gracious, and will show
compassion to whom I will show compassion."
EXODUS 33:19 NASB

Dear Father, in this passage, You address Moses. He pleaded for the Israelite people and asked You to show mercy, grace, and compassion. You were so impressed by Moses' sincere concern for his people that You let him see You. . .at least in part. You allowed him to see Your goodness. But You also told him that Your grace and compassion were of Your own free will and not because of anything Moses had said or done. Show me Your goodness, Father. Pour out Your grace and compassion on my life, not because I deserve it, but because I'm lost without Your great love.

How has God shown you His goodness,
His compassion, His grace, and His love?

My Sole Desire

"For what does it profit a man to gain the whole world and forfeit his soul?"

MARK 8:36 ESV

Dear Father, I don't consider myself to be a shallow or materialistic person. But there are things in my life that I long for, and sometimes I get a little obsessed with reaching those goals. But really, what does it matter? Aside from what matters for eternity, anything I accomplish in this life will wither away and disappear. The more time I spend focusing on earthly objectives, the less time I spend doing what really counts: pleasing You, reflecting Your love, and pointing others to You. I don't want to spend so much time chasing after silly dreams that I lose my soul in the process. My single aim, my sole desire, is to live for You.

What are some of your personal goals? Will they help you live out God's purpose for your life?

The Hard Way

*They offered him wine to drink, mixed with gall,
but when he tasted it, he would not drink it.*

MATTHEW 27:34 ESV

Dear Father, wine mixed with gall (bitter herbs) was a concoction that dulled the sense of pain. This was often given to suffering people to ease their way as they died. When Jesus realized what it was, He refused it. He knew our sin against You was severe, and it required a severe punishment. He endured every bit of pain and agony to make sure the full price was paid. In this, He showed great courage and commitment. Sometimes I'm tempted to take the easy way. While shortcuts have their place, sometimes they result in less than ideal outcomes. Give me courage and conviction to do things the hard way when that is what's required.

Have you ever been tempted to take the easy way, even if it wasn't the best way?

The Great Commission

"Go therefore and make disciples of all nations, baptizing them in the name of the Father and of the Son and of the Holy Spirit, teaching them to observe all that I have commanded you. And behold, I am with you always, to the end of the age."

MATTHEW 28:19–20 ESV

Dear Father, this passage is known as "the Great Commission." A commission is a command, instruction, or assignment. As I break down this passage, I wonder how well I'm following instructions. Am I making disciples? Am I teaching others to observe all Your commandments? Am I actively leading others to You? Help me fulfill my part in this commission, as I share Your love with those around me. Thank You for Your promise that You will be right beside me through every moment. You will never leave me, even when I face rejection from others. Give me courage and fortitude as I live out this commandment.

How well do you feel that you're following this commandment?

Disagreement

And there arose a sharp disagreement, so that they separated from each other. Barnabas took Mark with him and sailed away to Cyprus, but Paul chose Silas and departed, having been commended by the brothers to the grace of the Lord. And he went through Syria and Cilicia, strengthening the churches.

ACTS 15:39–41 ESV

Dear Father, relationships are difficult. We have differences of opinion, and everyone thinks they're right. You told us to live at peace with others as much as we're able. But sometimes, even when we do everything in our power, we still can't agree. This often leads to old friends going their separate ways, and that hurts. But this rift, between Paul and Barnabas, actually ended in two missionary journeys instead of one. More people were told about You because of it. Thank You for this reminder that You really do cause all things to work together for good for those who love You.

Have you done all you can to live at peace with others?

Happy in Heart

*Then on the twenty-third day of the seventh month
he sent the people to their tents, rejoicing and happy
in heart because of the goodness that the LORD had
shown to David, to Solomon, and to His people Israel.*

2 CHRONICLES 7:10 NASB

Dear Father, in this verse, Solomon sent the people home after the Feast of Dedication. They rejoiced and were happy because, through the years, You'd been so, so good to them. I can say the same thing! I can rejoice and be happy in my heart because You have shown Your goodness to me in countless ways. From the moment I drew my first breath, through my childhood, all the way to now, You have loved me. You never left me. And every day, despite trials that try to distract me, I see evidence of Your kindness. Thank You for Your all-consuming, never-ending love.

*Where is your focus today? On
your trials or on God's goodness?*

All Things Well

And they were astonished beyond measure,
saying, "He has done all things well. He even
makes the deaf hear and the mute speak."
MARK 7:37 ESV

Dear Father, there is no one more excellent than Your Son. Though I can never hope to match Him in love or grace or competence, I want to try. When people look at me, I want them to say, "She has done all things well." I want to give my best in every area because, as Your child, I know my actions reflect Your character to others. Help me excel in the areas that matter most to You. Help me pour out Your love, grace, mercy, forgiveness, and compassion on those You place in my path. When people see me, I want them to be astonished at Your love.

In what way can you pour out His
excellence on those around you?

Women of Prominence

*And some of them were persuaded and joined Paul
and Silas, as did a great many of the devout Greeks
and not a few of the leading women. . . . Many
of them therefore believed, with not a few Greek
women of high standing as well as men.*

ACTS 17:4, 12 ESV

Dear Father, "not a few" means many. These two verses
point out that many important women became early
converts to Christianity. During a time when women
were looked down on, Your Word points out that these
women of prominence played an important role in the
spread of the early Church. Their conversions likely
lifted some eyebrows and probably caused others to
consider the Christian faith for themselves. Throughout Your Word, You list women of influence. These
women held positions of power and inherited along
with their brothers. Whatever power and influence I
have, let me use it for You.

*In what ways do you have power and influence?
How can you use that to win others to Him?*

Diplomacy

*So Paul, standing in the midst of the Areopagus,
said: "Men of Athens, I perceive that in every way
you are very religious. . . . The God who made the
world and everything in it, being Lord of heaven
and earth, does not live in temples made by man,
nor is he served by human hands, as though he
needed anything, since he himself gives to all
mankind life and breath and everything."*

ACTS 17:22, 24–25 ESV

Dear Father, when addressing the Greeks, Paul didn't charge in like a bull, telling them they were pagans and insulting their beliefs. He began with a statement of respect. He used tact and diplomacy, and his approach earned him their listening ears. Many Greeks left their pagan ways to follow You, but they may not have if Paul had been rude or overbearing. Teach me to use tact and diplomacy as I relate to others, so they'll be open to hearing about You.

*Can you recall a time when you
could have used more tact?*

Influence

The soldiers' plan was to kill the prisoners,
lest any should swim away and escape. But
the centurion, wishing to save Paul, kept
them from carrying out their plan.

ACTS 27:42–43 ESV

Dear Father, things looked pretty grim for Paul in that moment. If not for the centurion, Paul would have been killed. But Your purpose will always be fulfilled! You placed that centurion there to aid Paul. Because of his power and influence, Paul lived to write many more books of the Bible. I can recall times in my own life when You placed people in my path to help me, just when it looked like all was lost. Thank You for those kind rescuers. Make me aware of others who may be struggling, who may need my kindness and influence as well.

Can you think of anyone who may need your
help? How do you think God wants you to help?

Stored Up

How great is Your goodness, which You have stored up for those who fear You, which You have performed for those who take refuge in You, before the sons of mankind! You hide them in the secret place of Your presence from the conspiracies of mankind; You keep them secretly in a shelter from the strife of tongues.

PSALM 31:19–20 NASB

Dear Father, when I think of storing things up, I think of an overcrowded closet filled with things I don't need anymore. But You're not a hoarder. Instead, You have countless good things, innumerable blessings, stored up for just the right time. You'll pour them out when they're most needed and will be most appreciated. These blessings are abundant and beyond measure, and You have them ready for those who love You, call on You, and try to please You. Today, Father, pour out Your blessings on me and on all those I love.

What kind of blessings do you hope God has for you? Tell Him, and trust His goodness.

True Purpose

He lived there two whole years at his own expense, and welcomed all who came to him, proclaiming the kingdom of God and teaching about the Lord Jesus Christ with all boldness and without hindrance.

ACTS 28:30–31 ESV

Dear Father, I don't think there were retirement plans in biblical days. Paul certainly didn't stop working. You want us to work until we can no longer work, don't You? Whether it's employment in a traditional job or working during our retirement years, our true purpose never sways: we are to be Your hands and feet here on earth. Forgive me for placing too much emphasis on my secular work, Father. Everything I have, every dime I make, every talent I possess—it's all given by You, and it's all to be used in a way that brings You glory. Show me what that should look like in my life.

What is the main emphasis of your life? What do you work for more than anything else?

Without Faith

And without faith it is impossible to please him, for whoever would draw near to God must believe that he exists and that he rewards those who seek him.
HEBREWS 11:6 ESV

Dear Father, I truly want to please You. But too often, I try to please You with good works, with achievements and kind deeds. Those things do please You, but only if I truly have faith in Your goodness, power, and love. Even pagans do good things. Even evil people make charitable donations or show an act of kindness occasionally. You want my heart. When I try to please You but inside I'm worried and anxious that You won't do what You promised, I'm showing a lack of faith. Help me grow a strong faith, Lord. I want everything about my life to make You smile.

Do you struggle with a lack of faith? Ask God to make your faith stronger.

Puffed Up

This "knowledge" puffs up, but love builds up.
1 CORINTHIANS 8:1 ESV

Dear Father, I spend too much time trying to be impressive. I read and study. I work hard to produce good results. Though it's hard to admit, I have a subtle, ugly pride that compels me to be the best, or at least better than those around me. And I always want to be right as well. When will I learn that You're more concerned about my heart being right than whether I win a competition or an argument? Teach me to love the way You love. Teach me to build others up and to be a kind, encouraging presence. Help me to lay aside my pride and to be more concerned about making others feel important than making myself feel important. Help me build others up.

Have you ever known someone who seemed "puffed up"? How did you feel when you were around that person?

Sun and Shield

*For the LORD God is a sun and shield; the LORD
gives grace and glory; He withholds no good
thing from those who walk with integrity.*

PSALM 84:11 NASB

Dear Father, You are my sun, giving light to my path.
You are my shield, protecting me in ways I may not even
be aware of. You pour out Your grace on my life! As I
consider my days, I can see that You haven't withheld
anything I've needed. I want to walk with integrity. As
I go about my business today, let me be a reflection of
Your glory, Your kindness, and Your love. Help me love
justice, mercy, and compassion, and give me humility
as I deal with others. I love You, Father. Thank You for
Your goodness.

*In what ways has God been your
sun and your shield? How has He
poured out His goodness on you?*

Healed

*And wherever he came, in villages, cities,
or countryside, they laid the sick in the
marketplaces and implored him that they might
touch even the fringe of his garment. And
as many as touched it were made well.*

MARK 6:56 ESV

Dear Father, I know these miracles were not just for one time and place. You are still the Healer, and anyone You choose can be healed at Your touch. This verse tells how You healed physical ailments, but You heal the spirit as well. I know You've placed Your healing power in me. Wherever I go, You place people in my path who need Your touch. They need a smile, a kind word, a show of compassion. Many of them are lonely and need a friend. Many feel invisible, and they need someone to see them. When people come near me, let them feel Your touch. Let my smile, my words, and my actions heal their hurting spirits and point them to Your love.

Who in your life needs a touch from God?

Let Them See You

They only were hearing it said, "He who used to persecute us is now preaching the faith he once tried to destroy." And they glorified God because of me.

GALATIANS 1:23–24 ESV

Dear Father, do others glorify You because of me? When they look at my life, do they see the miracle of Your presence? Do they see Your influence in my actions and attitudes? I hope so. Too often, my words and deeds could easily turn people away from You. May that never happen again, Lord. Make my life such a clear reflection of Your love that when others see me, they see You. I want to be a mirror of Your kindness and grace to those around me. Let them see all the marvelous things You've done in my life; let them see You.

Is your life a reflection of God's love? How can you show a clearer reflection?

Walk by the Spirit

But I say, walk by the Spirit, and you will not gratify the desires of the flesh. For. . .the desires of the Spirit are against the flesh, for these are opposed to each other, to keep you from doing the things you want to do. But if you are led by the Spirit, you are not under the law.
GALATIANS 5:16-18 ESV

Dear Father, when I walk by Your Spirit, I literally walk with You, close to You, all day long. Walking with You requires a spirit of praise. It calls for constant prayer. Someone who walks with Your Spirit truly knows and loves You. It's this kind of intimate relationship that keeps us from sin. I want to walk with You, Lord. I want You to hold my hand and guide me through every step, every word, every action.

What does it mean to you to "walk by the Spirit"?

More Than I Deserve

"Know, therefore, that the LORD your God is not
giving you this good land to possess because
of your righteousness, for you are a stubborn
people. Remember and do not forget how you
provoked the LORD your God to wrath in the
wilderness. From the day you came out of the
land of Egypt until you came to this place, you
have been rebellious against the LORD."

DEUTERONOMY 9:6-7 ESV

Dear Father, when I look at my life, I see how many times I've messed up. Like the Israelites, I can be stubborn and rebellious. But even at my best, I still don't deserve Your blessings. That's not why You bless me. The amazing love You pour out on my life is because of who You are, not because of anything I've done. You bless those who love You, despite our imperfections. I do love You with all my heart, Father. Thank You for blessing me far more than I deserve.

How has God blessed you today?

Roots and Fruit

But the fruit of the Spirit is love, joy, peace, patience,
kindness, goodness, faithfulness, gentleness,
self-control; against such things there is no law.
And those who belong to Christ Jesus have
crucified the flesh with its passions and desires.
GALATIANS 5:22–24 ESV

Dear Father, in the past I've focused on the fruits instead of the roots. But if the roots aren't healthy, the fruit won't grow. Am I impatient? I need to walk with Your Spirit. Have I been unkind? I need to spend more time with You. Your Holy Spirit produces the fruit. I can't produce it on my own. If I want more fruit, You are the answer. If I want healthier fruit, I must spend more time with You. Instead of wasting my time and energy focusing on being loving and patient and kind, I need to simply fall into You, every moment of each day.

Have you tried, unsuccessfully, to produce
good fruit in your life? Focus on the roots.

Seek Good

*Seek good and not evil, so that you may live; and
so may the LORD God of armies be with you, just as
you have said! Hate evil, love good, and establish
justice in the gate! Perhaps the LORD God of armies
will be gracious to the remnant of Joseph.*

AMOS 5:14–15 NASB

Dear Father, I know You are good. I love knowing that You
reward goodness in Your people. I was created in Your
image, but Satan wants to deform that image. He wants
to draw me into evil thoughts. He wants to fill my mind
with pettiness, anger, and envy. Help me fight him off,
Father! I want to be good like You. I want my thoughts,
words, and actions to reflect Your character, as I honor
You with everything I do.

*In what ways does your character reflect
God's goodness? Seek God today, and
let His goodness guide your actions.*

Much Fruit

"But those that were sown on the good soil are the ones who hear the word and accept it and bear fruit, thirtyfold and sixtyfold and a hundredfold."
MARK 4:20 ESV

Dear Father, let this be me. The proof that I belong to You is the fruit that I bear, and yet I can't bear fruit of my own accord. It only comes through You. The fruit shows up as I spend time with You, walking with You, reading Your Word and absorbing it into my life. Then, and only then, will I become a productive member of Your family. According to this verse, evidence lies in a bumper crop, not just a little fruit here and there. Transform my life into a fertile tree with strong roots. I want to bear Your fruit of love, goodness, patience, and kindness, in order to draw others to You.

Do you bear much fruit for Christ, or just a little? How can you become more fertile?

Who You Are

*Your ways, God, are holy. What god is as great as
our God? You are the God who performs miracles;
you display your power among the peoples.*
PSALM 77:13-14 NIV

Dear Father, I don't know why I walk around stressed, anxious, and worried about the future, when You hold such power. It seems the remedy to my frazzled thoughts is to stop, take some deep breaths, and remember who You are. You are holy. You are mighty. Your ways are far greater than my mind can imagine. Your ability to solve problems and perform miracles is as strong today as it ever was, and I am Your daughter. I can face the world with courage and confidence because You are my Father. I know You love me, and You will take care of me.

*Can you think of any problem that God can't
handle or that He can't use for good?*

More Than Talk

*For the kingdom of God is not a
matter of talk but of power.*
1 Corinthians 4:20 niv

Dear Father, this verse reminds me of the old saying "Put your money where your mouth is." Lots of people are big talkers, but they don't back up their talk with action. You, on the other hand, are as good as Your word. Your promises aren't just pretty comments; they're statements of fact, for those who believe. Though I don't always understand Your ways, I know You love me. I know You promised never to leave me or forsake me. I know Your peace is mine for the taking. And I know You will work out everything for my good. I can be confident in these promises because You are all-powerful. Thank You for backing up Your Word with action.

How has God fulfilled His promises to you?

Everlasting Covenant

"I will make an everlasting covenant with them that I will not turn away from them, to do them good; and I will put the fear of Me in their hearts, so that they will not turn away from Me."

JEREMIAH 32:40 NASB

Dear Father, Your promises aren't like man's promises. When a human makes a promise, circumstances may prevent fulfillment of that vow. But Your covenant is certain and unchanging. You promised You will not turn away from me, because I am Your child. You promised to do good for me every day of my life. Your love chases after me. When I feel far from You, it's often because I've run away from Your presence. Forgive me for doing that, Lord. Today and every day, place a holy reverence for You in my heart and keep me close to You.

In what ways has God's goodness followed you?

Powerful and Wise

*The wise prevail through great power, and those
who have knowledge muster their strength.*
PROVERBS 24:5 NIV

Dear Father, when I picture worldly power, I often think
of someone who is physically fit, with tight muscles,
superior strength, and endless endurance. Or I might
envision someone with a lot of money. But power is
different by Your standards. Your wisdom holds power.
And You promise to give wisdom to anyone who asks
(James 1:5). Though we can't all be Olympic athletes,
and most of us will never be independently wealthy,
we can have "great power." Thank You for making Your
power available to me through Your Word and Your Holy
Spirit. Make me wise, and teach me to use Your power
in a way that honors You.

*How does wisdom bring power?
How can you become wise?*

Strong in the Lord

Finally, be strong in the Lord and in his mighty power.
EPHESIANS 6:10 NIV

Dear Father, so many days I feel weak, like I can't take another step. I feel wimpy and defeated. But You have called me to be strong. How do I get there? How do I build spiritual muscle so I can stand against life's storms? How do I become powerful so I can fight evil and darkness and win? I know You don't want me to go through life as a victim, scared and defeated. You've created me in Your image, and You are powerful. You are wise and strong and victorious. Teach me, Father. Show me how to be strong, for myself and for others. I want Your mighty power to be displayed in my life for all to see.

What changes can you make in your life so you can be spiritually stronger?

Armor of God

*Put on the full armor of God, so that you can
take your stand against the devil's schemes.*
EPHESIANS 6:11 NIV

Dear Father, when You promised never to leave me or
forsake me, You didn't just mean You would walk with
me and hold my hand. You also meant that You wouldn't
leave me defenseless. You didn't create me to be some
wilting hothouse flower waiting to be rescued. You made
me to be a warrior, and You left me a full set of armor to
fight life's battles with. Too often, I leave my armor behind
and expect You to constantly come to my rescue. Teach
me to wear the armor well. Teach me to use each piece
with skill. I want to stand tall and proud, as a child of
the King. When I walk into a room, I want the enemy to
know that I'm a strong, powerful daughter of God.

Do you sometimes forget to wear your armor?

Who We're Fighting

For our struggle is not against flesh and blood, but against the rulers, against the authorities, against the powers of this dark world and against the spiritual forces of evil in the heavenly realms.

EPHESIANS 6:12 NIV

Dear Father, I get frustrated with other people, with my job, with my circumstances. I get sidetracked, and I see these people and things as my enemies. But other people aren't the enemy. Situations aren't the enemy. I am fighting in Your army, together with Your other children. Together, we battle Satan. We battle sin. We battle forces we will never see with our eyes. Yet the evil we're fighting is just as real as anything I can see and touch in the physical world. If I am to win against such forces, I must be fully equipped with every piece of armor You've provided. Make me powerful, and show me how to fight to win.

Have you lost focus of who the real enemy is?

Still Standing

Therefore put on the full armor of God, so that when the day of evil comes, you may be able to stand your ground, and after you have done everything, to stand.
 EPHESIANS 6:13 NIV

Dear Father, at times I've made the mistaken assumption that if I live for You, everything will be easy. You never promised that, did You? Instead, You said You'll make me strong. You'll make me powerful. You'll make me a warrior, and You'll supply the armor. What good is a warrior if there's no battle? And in any battle, there's a struggle. I'll sweat. I'll get banged and bruised and scraped. I'll most certainly feel the enemy's sting. But at the end of the fight, the winner is the one left standing. According to Your Word, when I wear Your full armor, I'll win. In the end, I'll stand.

What battles have left you battered and scarred? Are you still standing?

Pursuit

*Certainly goodness and faithfulness will follow
me all the days of my life, and my dwelling
will be in the house of the LORD forever.*
PSALM 23:6 NASB

Dear Father, this psalm is one of the most memorized passages in Your Word. But how often have I stopped to consider its meaning? Your goodness and faithfulness follow me! They pursue me. From the moment I drew my first breath until I take my final one, Your love actively chases me down. The thought overwhelms me. Because I'm Your child, my dwelling is in Your house, in Your presence, forever. The word *forever* indicates no ending, no beginning. I am already dwelling in Your presence; wherever I go, there You are! Thank You for pursuing me, Father. Help me pursue You as well. From the moment I wake up until I fall asleep, I want to chase after Your presence, Your goodness, and Your love.

How are you pursuing God today?

Peace, Truth, and Righteousness

*Stand firm then, with the belt of truth buckled around
your waist, with the breastplate of righteousness
in place, and with your feet fitted with the
readiness that comes from the gospel of peace.*
EPHESIANS 6:14–15 NIV

Dear Father, this passage describes three key pieces of
Your armor. You want me to wear the belt of truth. Your
Word is truth. Help me memorize Your Word and hide
it in my heart. And help me speak Your truth, with love,
into every situation. I need to wear the breastplate of
righteousness. When I'm in right standing with You, that
righteousness protects my heart from the worst of life's
blows. You also want my feet fitted with the Gospel of
peace. This peace wears like great shoes, so I'm ready
in any situation. I want to wear Your armor well, every
single day.

*Have you made good use of
these vital parts of God's armor?*

The Shield

*In addition to all this, take up the shield
of faith, with which you can extinguish
all the flaming arrows of the evil one.*
EPHESIANS 6:16 NIV

Dear Father, we fight a powerful enemy, and he has some pretty nasty weapons. To walk into battle without the proper armor is foolish. When we do that, we ask for flaming arrows to pierce our skin, all the way down to our souls. We can't possibly win such a battle. But You've provided the very best protection against this enemy: faith. I can hold up my faith like a shield against all sorts of attacks, and those arrows will immediately fall to the ground. Build my faith, Father, as a strong shield against the worst of life's assaults. Make me a strong warrior.

*Are you using your shield of faith
to fight life's battles, or do you
sometimes leave it behind?*

The Helmet and Sword

Take the helmet of salvation and the sword
of the Spirit, which is the word of God.
EPHESIANS 6:17 NIV

Dear Father, salvation through Your Son, Jesus Christ, is my helmet. It protects my head, my mind, my thoughts. Without a helmet, I'm an easy target, useless in battle. Thank You for my salvation that serves as a key piece of armor.

Your Word is the weapon You've provided. It's the sword, and it's the only offensive tool in the set. The rest of the armor is for protection, but Your Word actually does battle. It pierces the darkness and fells the enemy. I can't use this weapon unless I know what Your Word says. When I speak Your promises, Your power changes the course of the battle. When I speak Your Word, the enemy flees. Teach me Your Word, Father. Sear it on my heart so it's ready at every moment. Thank You for such a powerful weapon at my disposal.

How familiar are you with God's Word?

God's Presence

*Whenever the impure spirits saw him, they fell down
before him and cried out, "You are the Son of God."*

MARK 3:11 NIV

Dear Father, even the enemy knows Your power. Yet
sometimes I doubt You. How foolish of me to ever
question You. Forgive my unbelief, and strengthen
my faith. Make me a living, breathing example of Your
presence here on earth. When I walk into a room, I don't
care if people notice me or not. But Lord, let them notice
You. I want Your existence in my life to be so strong, so
clear, so obvious that people can't deny You. Like those
spirits, I want others to fall down and worship You when
they recognize Your existence in my life. Use me to draw
people to You so that You will be lifted up and glorified
and so that they will be saved.

*How can you increase God's presence and power
in your life? The more time you spend with
Him, the stronger His presence becomes.*

In the Land of the Living

*I certainly believed that I would see the goodness
of the LORD in the land of the living.*

PSALM 27:13 NASB

Dear Father, it's easy to get frustrated with the trials and storms of this life. In those times, I often think about heaven and how great it will be when I arrive. But Your goodness isn't for some faraway time and place. It's active right now, in the land of the living! You want me to experience Your kindness, Your glory, and Your love each day as I walk in Your presence. When life gets hard, hold tight to my hand. Remind me that You're right here, right now, and that You will see me through whatever life throws my way. And in the process, I know You'll surprise me with Your kindness; You'll astonish me with Your love.

*In what ways has God
proved His goodness today?*

Confidence

Therefore do not throw away your confidence,
which has a great reward. For you have need of
endurance, so that when you have done the will
of God you may receive what is promised.

HEBREWS 10:35-36 ESV

Dear Father, the author of Hebrews reminded readers of all they had endured for Christ. The Hebrew Christians had been publicly ridiculed for their faith. They'd been plundered because of it. They'd suffered greatly for associating with the name of Christ, and they had endured with confidence. Then, after they'd been through so much, some of them wanted to turn back. The author encouraged them to stay the course, to endure, to cling to their confidence and faith. I haven't been through anything close to what those early believers endured, yet I sometimes lose faith. Give me confidence, and help me endure to the end, Father.

What kinds of things cause you to lose
faith? Cling to your belief that God is
all-powerful and that He loves you.

Masterpiece

For you formed my inward parts; you knitted me together in my mother's womb. I praise you, for I am fearfully and wonderfully made. Wonderful are your works; my soul knows it very well.

PSALM 139:13-14 ESV

Dear Father, I've read this poetic psalm many times, yet it never gets old. The idea of it takes my breath away. The fact that You formed me, "knitted" me, while I was still in my mother's womb indicates You took such special care with me. You—the King of kings—thought I was a good idea. I praise You, Father, for giving me life. May I never squander this beautiful gift You've given. I want my every breath to please You. May every word, every thought, and every action be a delight to You.

Is there something about the way you're made that you don't like? Have you considered that you're God's masterpiece?

God Will Fight for You

"Be strong and courageous. Do not be afraid or dismayed before the king of Assyria and all the horde that is with him, for there are more with us than with him. With him is an arm of flesh, but with us is the LORD our God, to help us and to fight our battles." And the people took confidence from the words of Hezekiah king of Judah.

2 CHRONICLES 32:7–8 ESV

Dear Father, since the beginning of time, You've told Your people to be strong and courageous. In this passage, the people didn't need to fear the king of Assyria. He was strong, but You were stronger. In the same way, I don't need to fear any number of things that threaten my peace, my joy, and my well-being. I know You will help me. You'll fight my battles for me. Thank You, Father. I trust You completely.

What battles need fighting in your life right now? God will fight for you.

When Grace Meets Power

But he said to me, "My grace is sufficient for you,
for my power is made perfect in weakness." Therefore
I will boast all the more gladly of my weaknesses,
so that the power of Christ may rest upon me.

2 CORINTHIANS 12:9 ESV

Dear Father, there is so much to unpack in this one verse. First, Your grace is all I need. Your grace—something pure and holy, something I didn't earn and don't deserve—will see me through any situation, any weakness. Thank You for Your grace in my life. Next, Your power is made perfect in my weakness. When I'm strong, I risk not relying on You. But when I'm at the end of my strength, that's when I'm fully reliant on Your power. Remind me of this truth when I struggle, when I'm weak. That's the point where grace meets power. That's the point of victory.

How has God's power been made
perfect through your struggles?

Showing Love

*"So if you, despite being evil, know how to
give good gifts to your children, how much
more will your Father who is in heaven give
good things to those who ask Him!"*

MATTHEW 7:11 NASB

Dear Father, You know how I love the people You've
placed in my life. I try my best to show them kindness, compassion, and appreciation. I do things for no
reason, just to see them smile. But despite my best
intentions, I often fail. I grow impatient or lose my temper. I forget important days and special events. Still, I
hope those people know how much I love them. Your
love is so much better than flawed, human love. If I do
good things for those I care about, how much more will
You pour out Your goodness on me? Show me Your love
today, Father. Teach me to love others. And help me trust
in Your overwhelming kindness.

*How can you reflect God's amazing,
abundant love to others today?*

He Cares

And a leper came to him, imploring him, and kneeling
said to him, "If you will, you can make me clean."
Moved with pity, he stretched out his hand and
touched him and said to him, "I will; be clean."
MARK 1:40-41 ESV

Dear Father, Jesus had compassion on this man. He cared about the man's problems, and He healed him. I know You care about my problems as well. Teach me to come to You as this man did, with full confidence that You care and that You are able to do all things. Help me view others through a lens of compassion too. Help me see their hurts and their problems, and show me how to respond in a way that eases their burdens and lets them know that You care.

What problems do you need to bring to
Christ today? He cares, and He is able.

Birthright

*For God gave us a spirit not of fear but
of power and love and self-control.*
2 TIMOTHY 1:7 ESV

Dear Father, there are situations in my life that I have no control over. These circumstances often bring out the worst in me. I feel anxious and afraid. I lose my temper and lash out at others. But none of those responses are from You. Because I'm Your child, I've inherited Your character. I don't need to be afraid, because You've given me power. I don't need to lose my temper, because You've given me self-control. I can love others even when it's difficult, because Your love is in me. When life's storms surround me, remind me of who I am and whose I am. Remind me of my birthrights of power, love, and self-control.

*Have you tried to handle difficult situations
in your own power, instead of relying on
your birthright as a child of God?*

Access

This was according to the eternal purpose
that he has realized in Christ Jesus our Lord,
in whom we have boldness and access with
confidence through our faith in him.
EPHESIANS 3:11–12 ESV

Dear Father, in this passage, Paul wrote of God's calling and purpose for his life. He was given grace to preach Christ to the Gentiles. Though he suffered at times, he knew he didn't suffer alone. He could approach the King of kings at any time with boldness. He had full access to You, as one with a high calling. But he said "we." We includes me. I have full access to You, anytime I need You, because I'm important in Your kingdom. You've given me a calling and a purpose, and You're interested in everything that affects my life. Thank You for giving me such clearance and responsibility. May I serve You well.

Do you take advantage of the boldness and access you have with your Father, the King?

Draw Near

Let us then with confidence draw near to the throne of grace, that we may receive mercy and find grace to help in time of need.

HEBREWS 4:16 ESV

Dear Father, I hate to admit it, but sometimes I stage my prayers to say what I think You want to hear. I don't always approach You with full honesty, though I know You see right through my motives. When will I learn that I don't have to put on airs with You? You already know every weakness, every struggle. You love me, and You don't judge me harshly. Instead, You want to help me. When I come to You with my failures, You show grace. You pour out Your mercy. And You provide the help I need, every single time. Give me confidence in Your love for me. Good or bad, teach me to lay it all at Your feet.

Have you ever felt hesitant to talk to God about something you're feeling or experiencing or about a poor choice you've made?

Confident

For I am confident of this very thing, that
He who began a good work among you will
complete it by the day of Christ Jesus.
PHILIPPIANS 1:6 NASB

Dear Father, I love the reminder in this verse that You're not finished with me yet. Sometimes when I face an obstacle, it feels like it's the end of the story. But for You, those difficulties are simply plot twists. You allow those storms in my life to make me more like You: stronger, kinder, more compassionate, more confident in my status as Your child. When I feel discouraged by my circumstances, remind me that You'll bring things into play that I never thought possible in order to bring about Your plans for my victorious, happy ending. Thank You for the assurance that You're still working and that Your plans for me are good.

What circumstance in your life
leaves you feeling discouraged?
Take heart. God is not finished yet.

No Fear

So we can confidently say, "The Lord is my helper;
I will not fear; what can man do to me?"
HEBREWS 13:6 ESV

Dear Father, I'm guilty. I admit it. I do worry about what others can do to me. What if I don't get that job or that promotion? What if my children don't make the choices I want them to make? What if, what if, what if... The fears go on and on. But You didn't create me to be fearful. You created me to be powerful and confident. You created me to stand strong and be a warrior, knowing that You will help me. You will fight for me. There is nothing any human can do that can diminish my standing as Your child. Remind me to lift my head, hold my shoulders back, and look life in the face with confidence. I will not fear, for I know You are on my side.

What are you afraid of? God is bigger and more powerful than your worst fears.

The Noble Person

As for the scoundrel—his devices are evil; he plans wicked schemes to ruin the poor with lying words, even when the plea of the needy is right. But he who is noble plans noble things, and on noble things he stands.
ISAIAH 32:7-8 ESV

Dear Father, how many scoundrels do I know? It's easy to fall into step with people who gossip and slander, who take pleasure in harming those they don't agree with or don't like. As long as they're nice to me, it's hard to see them for who they are. Open my eyes to those whose words and actions are ungodly, and please don't let me become that kind of person. I want to be noble and godly. Make me like You, and let all my words and actions be born of love.

In what ways can you be noble to those around you?

Wait

Even youths shall faint and be weary, and young men shall fall exhausted; but they who wait for the LORD shall renew their strength; they shall mount up with wings like eagles; they shall run and not be weary; they shall walk and not faint.
ISAIAH 40:30–31 ESV

Dear Father, I'm weary. To be honest, I'm exhausted. I know the answer to this problem doesn't lie in getting more rest, though that certainly won't hurt. I can eat better, exercise, and take my vitamins, but somehow, I know I'll still end up tired and worn. The answer is to wait for You. Waiting means trusting that You will come through. It means believing, without doubt, that You will show up with all Your power and might and You will act. That kind of waiting brings excitement and expectation. It pumps up my adrenaline and keeps me going with anticipation. Teach me to wait, expecting, excited for what You're doing in my life.

What are you waiting on God to do? Wait with anticipation.

Fear Not!

Fear not, for I am with you; be not dismayed, for I am your God; I will strengthen you, I will help you, I will uphold you with my righteous right hand.
ISAIAH 41:10 ESV

Dear Father, how many times have I told my children not to be afraid? How many times did my own parents tell me the same thing? You truly are a loving parent, shushing me, comforting me, and reminding me that You're right here with me at all times. When life leaves me dismayed, I can rest in You. When circumstances overwhelm me, I can trust Your loving hand. When struggles leave me weak and afraid, I can find confidence and strength in Your presence. Thank You for never leaving me to fend for myself. No matter what, I will not be afraid. You are strong and powerful, and You walk right beside me.

What makes you fearful? Picture your almighty Father holding your hand, protecting you.

Intended for Good

"As for you, you meant evil against me, but God meant it for good in order to bring about this present result, to keep many people alive."
GENESIS 50:20 NASB

Dear Father, I often give other people way too much credit, thinking they wield a lot of power over my life. Others may have evil intent against me, but they don't hold any power against You. Just as You allowed Joseph's brothers to sell him into slavery, You might allow others to cause me temporary harm. But what those brothers saw as the end of Joseph's story was only the beginning. You allowed him to become a slave because You knew that ultimately that event would lead to his rise in power. This power allowed him to play a key role in saving the nation of Israel. When others try to bring me down, remind me that You, and You alone, will have the final say in my life.

What circumstance seems harmful to you right now? Trust God's good plan for your life.

Trust in the Lord

"Blessed is the man who trusts in the LORD, whose trust is the LORD."

JEREMIAH 17:7 ESV

Dear Father, I want to be blessed. Too often, my focus is on the blessings instead of on being blessable. You said that when I have faith, I am blessed. When I trust You, I am blessed. When You are pleased, You pour out good things on Your children. In Hebrews 11:6, You said that without faith it's impossible to please You. Grow my faith, Father. I'm not asking for the blessings, but rather for the opportunity to please You. I want my life to delight You and make You smile. Pleasing You is the best blessing I can hope for. Teach me to trust You.

In what areas is it hard for you to trust God? Spend time in His Word, soaking in His love and His promises. The better you know Him, the easier it is to trust Him.

Sing

And when they had sung a hymn,
they went out to the Mount of Olives.
MATTHEW 26:30 ESV

Dear Father, I love that they sang a hymn together that night. It was the night of Jesus' betrayal, the night that would begin that awful day of His crucifixion. Christ knew what was coming. Yet He didn't freak out or snap at His friends or melt into a nervous breakdown. Instead, He held a worship service. He sang. He prayed. And when His friends left Him, He prayed alone. He spent some of the most difficult hours of His life in communion with You. When I face storms and trials in my own life, remind me of Jesus' example. When I think I can't go on, remind me to sing.

What difficulties do you face right now?
Can you think of a song or hymn
that brings you closer to God?

Be Strong and Courageous

*"Have I not commanded you? Be strong
and courageous. Do not be frightened,
and do not be dismayed, for the LORD your
God is with you wherever you go."*
JOSHUA 1:9 ESV

Dear Father, some people think I'm strong and courageous. But deep down, I struggle with fear. Fear of failure. . .fear of my circumstances. . .fear of the future. Fear is the belief that something bad will happen. But You promised to be with me wherever I go. If things go the way I want them to, You are there. If my worst fears come true, You are there. Even in the midst of horrible situations, You've given me everything I need to be strong and fearless. You've given me the full armor of God. You've given me Your presence. And You've given me the confidence that comes from being Your child.

*Do you feel strong and courageous?
Why or why not?*

A Great Story

And when all our enemies heard of it, all the nations around us were afraid and fell greatly in their own esteem, for they perceived that this work had been accomplished with the help of our God.

NEHEMIAH 6:16 ESV

Dear Father, sometimes You allow Your children to endure difficult situations so You can show off. If everything were all rosy, if we only walked in lovely, flower-strewn meadows, You wouldn't have a chance to show Your power. But when we're put in the position of underdog and You save the day, people know. They see that You rescued Your children in a way that only You can. Those miracles make for such great story lines, Father. When I find myself in a difficult situation, remind me that You're setting things up for an amazing victory. I can't wait to see how You'll come through for me next time.

How has God shown His greatness in your life?

For Good

And we know that God causes all things to work together for good to those who love God, to those who are called according to His purpose.

ROMANS 8:28 NASB

Dear Father, life is hard. Sometimes, I don't know if I can continue the climb. Other people and life's circumstances leave me battered and bruised, wondering if I can take another step. But one look back at my life provides proof that You are good and that You're always working on my behalf. You know my heart, Lord, and You know I love You. I want to live out Your purpose for my life. Because of that, I have confidence that You will turn every trial into triumph. I trust Your goodness and Your love for me. I can't wait to see what You'll do.

How has God worked things out for good in your past? Trust that He's still working on your behalf.

Trustworthy

*These are the men whom the LORD
commanded to divide the inheritance for
the people of Israel in the land of Canaan.*
NUMBERS 34:29 ESV

Dear Father, You chose these men to make sure everyone got their fair portion of land. You chose them because You trusted them to do the right thing. What an honor! I want to be a person You can trust. When temptations run high, I want to behave in a way that honors You. Whether in public or private, when everyone is watching or no one is watching, I want to please You. As I go through my day today, walk with me. Guide my steps. Help me be trustworthy in all that I do. When others look at my life, I want them to see You.

*What has God entrusted you with?
Ask Him to help you do the right thing,
even when no one is watching.*

Cause and Effect

And the effect of righteousness will be peace, and the result of righteousness, quietness and trust forever.
ISAIAH 32:17 ESV

Dear Father, an effect is the direct result of something. Here, You explain clearly that the result, or effect, of righteousness is peace. How many times have I asked You for peace? How many times have I longed for serenity? I can have that by walking close to You. The closer I am to You, the more my thoughts and actions please You. And the more I please You, the more righteous I become, which leads to that quiet peace I so long for. It's a peace that's not dependent on circumstances. Instead, it comes from knowing that You love me beyond measure and that You're in control. Keep me close to You today. Help me grow in righteousness, and let my life reflect the serenity that only comes from knowing You.

In what areas of your life do you wish you had more peace?

Full Attention

And this is the confidence that we have
toward him, that if we ask anything
according to his will he hears us.
1 JOHN 5:14 ESV

Dear Father, it's pretty incredible to have an audience with a king anytime I want it. Incredible or not, it's my reality. You've promised that because I'm Your child, I have full access to You. I can talk to You about anything, no matter how big or small, and You'll listen. You don't listen the way so many today listen. You're not on Your cell phone, scrolling through social media, nodding occasionally to make me think You're paying attention. Nope. When I talk to You, You lean forward and hang on every word. Thank You for loving me, for seeing me as important, and for listening to my prayers with Your full attention.

Do you ever wonder if God
hears your prayers? He does.

What It Means to Love

So we have come to know and to believe the love
that God has for us. God is love, and whoever
abides in love abides in God, and God abides in
him. By this is love perfected with us, so that we
may have confidence for the day of judgment,
because as he is so also are we in this world.
1 JOHN 4:16–17 ESV

Dear Father, it really is that simple, isn't it? You are love. The more time I spend with You, the more like You I become. The more like You I am, the more loving I am to the people around me. Love is a natural by-product of spending time with You. I want that, Father. I want Your love to be so thick in my life that others can feel it when I walk into a room. Teach me to see people through Your eyes. Teach me what it means to love.

How does time with God change
the way you love others?

Perfect Gifts

Every good thing given and every perfect gift is
from above, coming down from the Father of lights,
with whom there is no variation or shifting shadow.

JAMES 1:17 NASB

Dear Father, I know every good thing is from You. You overwhelm me with Your love, and You shower me with more blessings than I can count. I especially love the last part of this verse: "With whom there is no variation." You never change! Every good thing in my life is from You, and every day I draw breath, You'll continue to chase after me with Your love. You pursue me with kindness and blessings because that's who You are. It's in Your nature to give good and perfect gifts, and You delight in showering them on Your children. Thank You for Your eternal, pursuing love, Father. It makes me smile, all the way down to my soul.

What good thing has God done for you recently? He has countless more wonderful things in store for your life.

My Confidence

For the LORD will be your confidence and
will keep your foot from being caught.
PROVERBS 3:26 ESV

Dear Father, I can be pretty clumsy. It seems I'm constantly getting my "foot caught," as this verse says. I'm always stumbling, messing up, or putting that foot in my mouth! I've figured out that the less time I spend with You, the more often those mishaps happen. *You* steady my gait and keep me from stumbling. Whether those snares are my own doing or traps others have set for me, You keep me from being caught. But I can't rely on that confidence if I wander from Your presence. My confidence comes from staying close to You. My strength comes from spending time with You. Forgive me for ever walking away and for neglecting our relationship. Draw me close, and capture me with Your love. I need You every minute, every day.

How does the Lord give you confidence?

In His Confidence

Do not envy a man of violence and do not choose any of his ways, for the devious person is an abomination to the LORD, but the upright are in his confidence.

PROVERBS 3:31–32 ESV

Dear Father, to be in someone's confidence means that person trusts you. It means they share things with you they don't share with others. I love that the upright are in Your confidence. To be upright means to be honorable, moral, and conscientious. It means to be God-fearing and God-pleasing. Sometimes it's tempting to try to gain acceptance from the "popular" people of the world. But if those people aren't godly, I don't want their acceptance. I want to be upright, Father. I want to be the kind of person You trust. I want You to show me things through Your eyes. I want You to share Your heart with me. Take me into Your confidence, Lord.

Would you rather be in close confidence with ungodly people or with God?

In Whom Do I Trust?

Some trust in chariots and some in horses,
but we trust in the name of the LORD our God.
PSALM 20:7 ESV

Dear Father, in the psalmist's day, chariots and horses signified a big army. They showed military power and political strength. But even the biggest army is no match for You. Today the psalmist might write, "Some trust in money and some in accomplishments." Some might trust in family background or in having the right friends. It doesn't matter where I place my confidence. . .if it's not in You, it's not well placed. Forgive me for having faith in people or things that will fail me. I trust You, Father. My assurance is found in You alone. You are stronger than any giant, more powerful than any army. I'm so grateful to be Your child.

What are you tempted to put
your faith in, other than God?

Yet I Will Be Confident

Though an army encamp against me,
my heart shall not fear; though war arise
against me, yet I will be confident.

PSALM 27:3 ESV

Dear Father, too much of my life has been ruled by fear. You didn't create me to be fearful, did You? No matter how big the problem is, You are bigger. And no matter what I face, You are right by my side. My confidence comes from knowing Your power, Your might, and Your overwhelming, passionate love for me. Why should I be afraid? Your love for me is fierce and protective. You will fight for me. Not only that, but You've already equipped me to fight for myself. You don't want me to be a spectator in my own life! You want me right in the middle of the action, proving my strength as a child of the Most High God. Thank You for being my confidence so I don't have to be afraid.

What problem are you facing
that makes you feel afraid?

Stay the Course

For our momentary, light affliction is producing for us an eternal weight of glory far beyond all comparison.

2 CORINTHIANS 4:17 NASB

Dear Father, this verse reminds me of a strenuous workout program. When I'm out of shape or when I've gained a few pounds, I have to sweat to get back into shape. It's not always fun while I'm doing it; but over time, that discipline makes me feel better and gives me a healthier, stronger body. In the same way, You put me through spiritual workouts. I face difficulties that aren't fun when I'm going through them. But over time—as I practice faith, trust, and obedience to Your Word—I become like You. And being like You is truly glorious, beyond comparison to any earthly thing. Help me along, and give me strength and endurance to stay the course.

What is your momentary affliction? Stay the course. It will be worth it in the end.

All Things

I can do all things through
him who strengthens me.
PHILIPPIANS 4:13 ESV

Dear Father, I don't feel like I can do all things. Many days, I feel inadequate to accomplish even the most basic tasks. But when I feel that way, I'm usually trying to do things on my own. Oh, I may say a perfunctory prayer, but I'm still relying on my own strength and my own abilities to get things done. When I let go and fall into Your grace, something strange and beautiful happens. When I let go of my expectations and just let You have Your way, it's like I grow wings. I experience a new freedom in knowing I don't have to be good enough or strong enough or talented enough. You are all those things for me. All I need to do is trust You, and Your strength becomes my own.

What have you struggled to
accomplish on your own?

Love and Faithfulness

Let love and faithfulness never leave you; bind
them around your neck, write them on the tablet
of your heart. Then you will win favor and a
good name in the sight of God and man.

PROVERBS 3:3-4 NIV

Dear Father, I love the picture of tying love and faithfulness around my neck. It's kind of like attaching a key or name tag to a young child so they won't lose it. Faith pleases You, and love conquers all. When I hold love and faithfulness close, when I live and breathe and operate within those parameters, I make You smile. I find favor in Your eyes, and You bless me with success, peace, joy, and good relationships. Help me remain faithful to Your Word today. Help me love You and others with passion and purpose. Teach me to write Your ways on my heart so they never leave me.

Have you lost your faith or your ability
to love others? Ask God to help you
hold faithfulness and love close.

The Power of God

And I was with you in weakness and in fear and much trembling, and my speech and my message were not in plausible words of wisdom, but in demonstration of the Spirit and of power, so that your faith might not rest in the wisdom of men but in the power of God.
1 CORINTHIANS 2:3–5 ESV

Dear Father, poor Paul. I can relate to his words here. Though he was a great writer, apparently he wasn't a dynamic speaker. He was going through some things in his personal life that caused him much stress. Yet he didn't worry much about what he couldn't do. Instead, he found confidence in You. The wisdom he preached wasn't his own wisdom; it came from Your Holy Spirit. When I operate in Your power, I don't have to worry about a lack of ability or talent or prestige. When I am weak, Your strength shines.

In what areas do you feel inadequate?

Give Me Faith

Now faith is the assurance of things hoped for, the conviction of things not seen.
HEBREWS 11:1 ESV

Dear Father, I live in a see-it-to-believe-it world. I say I have faith, but I often live as if I don't. I hope, but I don't have assurance of the things I hope for. My convictions waver when I'm asked to act on things I can't see, things I'm not sure about. But the author of Hebrews wrote of a powerful faith. Give me this kind of faith, Father! Where there is doubt, give me certainty. Where there are questions, give me passionate conviction. Help me stand with confidence in Your power and love. When life throws chaos into my path, help me face it with courage, knowing for certain that You will see me through.

When it comes to your faith in God, are you assured of things you hope for and convinced of things you can't see?

About Discipline

For they disciplined us for a short time as seemed best to them, but He disciplines us for our good, so that we may share His holiness.

Hebrews 12:10 NASB

Dear Father, thank You for this reminder that even though the best of parents will get it wrong sometimes, You never will. You know every detail of my future, and You allow me to go through things that will best prepare me to run a winning race. Your goal isn't that I'm rich or successful, or even that I'm always happy. Instead, You want me to be like You: holy, set apart for Your high calling. I know the good plans You have for me are beyond my comprehension. I know discipline isn't about punishment; it's about preparation. Thank You for loving me enough to discipline me so I'll become exactly who You created me to be.

In what ways do you feel that God is trying to discipline you right now? Trust His motives. He loves you beyond measure.

The First One to Call

*It is better to take refuge in the LORD than
to trust in man. It is better to take refuge
in the LORD than to trust in princes.*
PSALM 118:8-9 ESV

Dear Father, sometimes when I have a problem and I
need help, I mentally scroll through all my family, friends,
and acquaintances. Who do I know that can help with
this problem? While it's not necessarily bad to rely on
others, they should never be my first source of comfort
or relief. When I need a refuge, You are the only place
to turn. People are flawed. They get busy, and they might
forget me. You, on the other hand, are strong, powerful,
and eternal in Your love for me. Next time I need help,
before I pick up my phone to call a friend, remind me
to run to You.

*Who is the first person you
call when you're in trouble?*

Serving with Joy

*"And whoever would be first among you must be your
slave, even as the Son of Man came not to be served
but to serve, and to give his life as a ransom for many."*
MATTHEW 20:27-28 ESV

Dear Father, I don't want to be anyone's servant, much
less their slave. I get annoyed and frustrated when I feel
used and taken advantage of. What You call me to do
goes against everything in my human nature. You want
me to put others first and put myself last. Yet, You weren't
a doormat. You didn't let others push You around. Teach
me to find balance, Father. I want to serve others out of
love, with joy. Yet I still want to exhibit the confidence
that comes from being Your daughter. I want to lay down
my life as Jesus did, by choice, to bring others to You.

*How can you serve others without
allowing them to walk on you?*

Reverence

In the fear of the LORD one has strong confidence,
and his children will have a refuge. The fear
of the LORD is a fountain of life, that one may
turn away from the snares of death.
PROVERBS 14:26–27 ESV

Dear Father, You've taught me not to fear anything in this world. But fearing You is another story, isn't it? I know You love me, so I never have to fear that You'll harm me in any way. But Your power and authority are beyond measure. I should have a deep respect, an awe-filled reverence, for who You are. You demand that kind of deference from Your children. When I honor You this way, You infuse me with Your confidence. You promise a safe place in Your arms. You give me a fountain of life, and You protect me from harm. Teach me to reverence You, Father.

Do you reverence God, or do you make
decisions without considering Him?

Cornerstone

For it stands in Scripture: "Behold, I am laying in Zion a stone, a cornerstone chosen and precious, and whoever believes in him will not be put to shame."
1 PETER 2:6 ESV

Dear Father, the cornerstone is sometimes called the foundation stone. It's the first stone that is laid in a brick or stone building. Every other stone is laid in reference to the cornerstone. That one stone determines the position of the entire structure. Jesus Christ is the cornerstone for the church. He is chosen and precious. I am but one small stone in the building, but every breath I take and each decision I make should be in reference to Your Son. Christ alone should determine my place and position in this life. Thank You for allowing me to be a part of Your amazing structure.

How closely do you reference Christ, the cornerstone, in the way you set your life?

Give Thanks

*"When you have eaten and are satisfied,
you shall bless the LORD your God for the
good land which He has given you."*
DEUTERONOMY 8:10 NASB

Dear Father, You've been so generous with me. I'm surrounded by Your blessings, so much so that I take them for granted. Forgive me for enjoying the good things You've provided without thanking You for them. I'm sorry for being preoccupied with my own thoughts and forgetting to acknowledge Your goodness. I'm sorry for thinking I earned or deserved any gift that comes from Your hand. Thank You for every good thing in my life, from the air I breathe to the people I love, and so many other blessings. I praise You, and I acknowledge that every beautiful thing I enjoy is from You.

*What good things have you taken
for granted? Make a list of your
blessings and thank God for them.*

Childlike

*"Whoever humbles himself like this child is
the greatest in the kingdom of heaven."*

MATTHEW 18:4 ESV

Dear Father, humility can be hard for an adult. We're taught to be strong and self-confident. Those are biblical qualities, but they can easily get mixed with pride. Christ was strong and self-confident, but He was also humble. He placed Himself completely under Your authority and was obedient even to death. He put others' needs before His own. He didn't get upset easily, and when He did, it was because Your character or purpose had been assaulted. Teach me to be humble. Give me the confidence to love with abandon, like a child. Teach me to trust You completely and to place myself under Your authority. And teach me to put others' needs before my own. Let there be less of me and more of You.

*What does it mean to be both confident
and humble? Which of those qualities
do you need help with the most?*

With All Your Heart

Trust in the LORD with all your heart,
and do not lean on your own understanding.
In all your ways acknowledge him, and
he will make straight your paths.
PROVERBS 3:5–6 ESV

Dear Father, I try to do this. I really do. But there are so many things here, in this life, that I don't understand. I don't know why there's so much evil in the world. I don't know why people are mean. I don't know why You created me the way You did, with so many flaws and weaknesses. I don't know why there is disease or why so many in this world are hurting and hungry. But in the midst of it all, I trust You. I know those difficult things will one day pass away and only Your love will remain. Because I trust You, I will consult You for all my decisions. Thank You for guiding me through this weary, hurting world.

In what areas is it hard for you to trust God?

Chosen

*Just as He chose us in Him before the foundation
of the world, that we would be holy and blameless
before Him. In love He predestined us to adoption
as sons and daughters through Jesus Christ
to Himself, according to the good pleasure of
His will, to the praise of the glory of His grace,
with which He favored us in the Beloved.*

EPHESIANS 1:4-6 NASB

Dear Father, this passage overwhelms me. I can hardly
wrap my head around it. You chose me, before You even
created the world? Way back then, You already knew
me by name. You decided You wanted me and would
adopt me as Your daughter through Christ. You did this
because it brought You pleasure! You loved me that
much. I can't understand this, but I'm truly grateful for
Your overwhelming love. Thank You for wanting me.

Did you know God smiles when He thinks of you?

Remind Me

*For we are His workmanship, created in Christ
Jesus for good works, which God prepared
beforehand so that we would walk in them.*
EPHESIANS 2:10 NASB

Dear Father, I forget this sometimes. I forget that You created me with a purpose. I'm not just a random product of cells and DNA. You planned my life with specific things for me to accomplish. Those tasks are all good works designed to help others, show love, and point them to You. You placed me in the exact place You need me so I can live out my part of Your plan. Remind me, as I go about my day, to do good works. Remind me to be patient, to show kindness, to be generous, and to smile. Remind me to show grace where it's not deserved. Remind me to love.

*What good works does God have planned for you?
Who around you needs to be shown His love?*

Tell Everyone!

They will burst forth in speaking of Your abundant goodness, and will shout joyfully of Your righteousness.
PSALM 145:7 NASB

Dear Father, this verse is a statement of how things should be. . .but not necessarily how they are. Those who love You, those who eagerly accept all Your generous gifts, should be overwhelmed by Your goodness. We should think about You all the time. We should be talking about You to anyone who will listen. We should be so filled with gratitude that it flows out of us. My thanksgiving should be fueling an uncontrollable urge to praise You, both out loud and in my heart, and to share Your goodness with everyone around me. Today and every day, let the "should be" become a reality. I can't wait to share Your bountiful love.

What good things has God poured out on your life? Have you told anyone about it?

Dwell in Me

Christ Jesus Himself. . .in whom you also are being built together into a dwelling of God in the Spirit.
EPHESIANS 2:20, 22 NASB

Dear Father, I want to be Your dwelling place. Too often, I invite things into my life that aren't befitting a King. I watch things on TV and social media that don't honor You. I listen to gossip and slander, and I say and do things that hurt people. Why do I use my mind and body to disrespect You, when I want nothing more than to honor You? Dwell in me, Father. Change me from the inside out. Decorate the walls of my life with the fruit of the Spirit and with good works that announce Your presence. When people are near me, let them feel You. Dwell in me, Lord.

Does your lifestyle invite God's presence? Based on your choices, does He feel welcome in your life?

Inclusive

And He came and preached peace to you who were far away, and peace to those who were near; for through Him we both have our access in one Spirit to the Father. So then you are no longer strangers and foreigners, but you are fellow citizens with the saints, and are of God's household.

EPHESIANS 2:17–19 NASB

Dear Father, the word *inclusion* is a popular one in our culture. It gets discussed on daily talk shows and on blogs and social media like it's a new concept. But You were inclusive long before I was born. You called Your people—Israel—to be Your own. But You also called the Gentiles. You didn't want to exclude anyone from Your love. Teach me Your kind of inclusiveness, Father. Help me see all people as objects of Your love. Help me show them Your kindness and grace. Make my life a magnet of Your presence, drawing all people to You.

Can you think of someone who is on the outside and needs to be included?

Power Source

"I will give you the keys of the kingdom of heaven, and whatever you bind on earth shall be bound in heaven, and whatever you loose on earth shall be loosed in heaven."
MATTHEW 16:19 ESV

Dear Father, I believe those keys You spoke of here are Your words. Your Word holds power. When I immerse myself in Your Word, that power seeps into my life. I know this is one of those beautiful mysteries of faith. When I am in perfect alignment with Your will, You unleash Your power in me. When I try to use that power for selfish reasons or in ways that don't line up with Your will, the power line is broken. I want to be a conduit of Your power here on earth so others can see how wonderful and awesome You are.

How much time do you spend connecting with the Power Source each day?

Equipped

And He gave some as apostles, some as prophets,
some as evangelists, some as pastors and teachers,
for the equipping of the saints for the work of
ministry, for the building up of the body of Christ.
EPHESIANS 4:11–12 NASB

Dear Father, often when I read this verse, I focus on the idea that we all have different gifts. But today I want to zone in on that phrase "for the equipping of the saints for the work of ministry." I am a saint because I am Your child. You have provided everything I need for ministry. No matter what I do for a living, I am called to do Your work. Sometimes I fail to carry out my calling because I doubt myself. But You've equipped me! Give me confidence in my ability to carry out whatever You have planned for my life.

Do you feel that God has called you to do
something specific? He will give you everything
you need to accomplish His purpose.

Love

Beloved, let's love one another; for love is from God, and everyone who loves has been born of God and knows God. The one who does not love does not know God, because God is love.

1 JOHN 4:7–8 NASB

Dear Father, I've known people I might describe as loving. But You're not just *loving*, are You? You are *love*. The very word is a synonym for God Almighty. Because You live in my heart, love lives there. When I fail to treat people with love, I'm actually denying Your residence in my life. Forgive me, Father! Teach me to love like You love. When others look at me, let them see a picture of You. I want Your love to be so all-consuming in my life that when I walk into a room, the temperature changes and people feel Your presence. Thank You for being love and for teaching me what that means.

Do you know someone who is hard to love? Ask God to live out His love through you.

Love, Beginning and End

But speaking the truth in love, we are to grow up in all aspects into Him who is the head, that is, Christ, from whom the whole body, being fitted and held together by what every joint supplies, according to the proper working of each individual part, causes the growth of the body for the building up of itself in love.
EPHESIANS 4:15-16 NASB

Dear Father, the first part of this passage speaks of love. The last word of this passage is *love.* All the stuff in the middle discusses how we should fit and work together as the body of Christ. When we're sandwiched in love, everything works as it should. But without love, things don't fit. People disagree, feelings get hurt, and not much gets accomplished. Help me start and end each day, each conversation, each interaction with Your love.

Can you think of a situation that needs to be sandwiched in love?

Worthy

Therefore I, the prisoner of the Lord, urge you to walk in a manner worthy of the calling with which you have been called, with all humility and gentleness, with patience, bearing with one another in love, being diligent to keep the unity of the Spirit in the bond of peace.

EPHESIANS 4:1–3 NASB

Dear Father, as I read these words, I can't help but think of times I don't "walk in a manner worthy of the calling." But You didn't just call me. You equipped me. You've given me everything I need to act in humility, with gentleness, patience, and love. Through Your Holy Spirit, I have what is necessary to live in unity and peace with those around me. Though others may or may not live according to Your will, I want to do my part. Help me live in a way that's pleasing to You and that's worthy of a person who is called Your child.

Are you living in a way that is fitting for a child of God?

Be Kind

Be kind to one another, compassionate,
forgiving each other, just as God in
Christ also has forgiven you.

EPHESIANS 4:32 NASB

Dear Father, this is such a pretty verse. It sounds so nice when I read it. Living it out? That's another story. I'm happy to be kind when others are kind or when they do what I want them to. But when they annoy me or frustrate me, I often respond in anger. It's easy to have compassion on a down-and-out stranger. But when someone I know hasn't followed my advice, I have a tendency to feel like they got what they deserved. I don't know why I'm so stingy with grace, when You've been so generous with me. Forgive me, Father, and help me love others the way You love me.

In what situations and with what people do you struggle to be kind, compassionate, and forgiving?

Imitating God

Therefore be imitators of God,
as beloved children.
EPHESIANS 5:1 NASB

Dear Father, when I was a little girl, I acted just like my mother. I practiced walking like her. I answered the phone like her. I dressed up in her clothes and played with her makeup on. I thought she was beautiful, and I wanted to be just like her. Sometimes I'd imitate my father. I'd wear his boots and coat and talk in a deep voice. This behavior delighted my parents! I know You're delighted when I imitate You. I'm Your child, and You love it when I act like You. Help me practice walking like You, talking like You, and speaking with Your voice of kindness, love, and compassion. I love You with all my heart, and I want to be just like You.

How can you imitate God today?
See how many ways you can
share His love with others.

Boundaries

"You shall follow my rules and keep my statutes and walk in them. I am the LORD your God. You shall therefore keep my statutes and my rules; if a person does them, he shall live by them: I am the LORD."

LEVITICUS 18:4–5 ESV

Dear Father, I know that all Your statutes are from love. Sin destroys us. It leads to broken relationships and broken lives. Before sin entered the world, we lived in perfect communion with You and with each other. But when Adam and Eve chose to go against Your rules, they entered a place of death and destruction. You hate sin because You hate what it does to Your children. That's why You gave us boundaries—to keep us safe. Thank You for loving me enough to show me Your boundaries. I want to obey You in everything I do.

Which of God's laws do you have a hard time keeping? Ask Him to help you.

The Accuser

At that time Jesus went through the grainfields on the Sabbath. His disciples were hungry and began to pick some heads of grain and eat them. When the Pharisees saw this, they said to him, "Look! Your disciples are doing what is unlawful on the Sabbath."

MATTHEW 12:1-2 NIV

Dear Father, the Pharisees were looking for something to accuse Jesus and His disciples of. They'd been doing Your work, and they were tired and hungry. Yet the Pharisees were quick to criticize. Satan is the accuser. When we look for something to criticize in others, we align ourselves with Satan. You show grace despite our flaws, but Satan wants to condemn us. When Satan accuses me, remind me to silence him. And when I criticize others, remind me that Satan is the source of harsh judgment. Thank You for treating me with grace and compassion. Help me reflect that kind of attitude toward others.

Have you ever been judged harshly? Have you been guilty of judging others harshly?

Turn On the Light!

For at one time you were darkness, but now you are light in the Lord. Walk as children of light (for the fruit of light is found in all that is good and right and true), and try to discern what is pleasing to the Lord.

EPHESIANS 5:8–10 ESV

Dear Father, my human, sinful nature placed me in the dark. I've noticed that unsavory creatures like to play in the dark. . .rats, roaches, even thieves. But when the light gets turned on, those creatures scurry. Light makes them uncomfortable, and they want to hide. When I became Your child, Your light entered my life, and it lives inside me. Help me walk as a child of light. Help me live in a way that is good and true and pure. Wherever I go, let Your love pierce through. Let darkness hide from Your presence when I enter a room. I want to be Your light in this dark world.

Are ungodly people ever uncomfortable in your presence?

Time Management

Look carefully then how you walk, not as unwise but as wise, making the best use of the time, because the days are evil. Therefore do not be foolish, but understand what the will of the Lord is.
EPHESIANS 5:15–17 ESV

Dear Father, "the days are evil." That's a great way to describe what's happening in the world right now. Everywhere I look, there is anger. There's social and political unrest. There's much division and little unity. Now, more than ever, I need Your wisdom. I need to make every day, every minute count for Your kingdom because I feel our time is growing short. Make Your will clear for my life, Father, and help me walk in wisdom, godliness, and love. I don't want to waste a single day. As long as I have breath in this world, let me honor You.

How do you feel that God wants you to use your time here?

Abounding Love

*And it is my prayer that your love may abound more
and more, with knowledge and all discernment,
so that you may approve what is excellent, and
so be pure and blameless for the day of Christ.*

PHILIPPIANS 1:9–10 ESV

Dear Father, Paul's prayer for the Philippians is what
I want for my own life as well. In his first letter to the
Corinthians, he spoke of love. He said that out of faith,
hope, and love—all beautiful traits—the greatest is love. I
want my love to abound more and more. Show me what
that looks like, Father. Show me what it means to truly
love the unlovable, to be kind when others are rude, to
show grace when it's not reciprocated. I want to love with
a joyful attitude. Give me an understanding heart, and
help me see others the way You see them.

*Does your heart abound with love,
even for those who aren't lovable?*

Power

Now to Him who is able to do far more abundantly
beyond all that we ask or think, according
to the power that works within us, to Him be
the glory in the church and in Christ Jesus to
all generations forever and ever. Amen.

EPHESIANS 3:20-21 NASB

Dear Father, every time I read this passage of scripture,
I'm overwhelmed by Your magnitude. I've felt Your love
in my life, but You're able to do more than I can think or
imagine! You are so great, so amazing, so wonderful that
my mind can't even scratch the surface. But I want to
know You more, Father. I want to spend my life learning
about Your goodness, Your kindness, Your mercy, and
Your love. Expand my understanding. Live out Your
power in my life. Today and every day, I will glorify You.
With every breath, I will praise You and thank You for
being who You are.

Have you ever tried to imagine God's power?
Now picture that power alive inside of you.

Seek God First

*And David inquired of the LORD, "Shall I
pursue after this band? Shall I overtake them?"
He answered him, "Pursue, for you shall
surely overtake and shall surely rescue."*

1 SAMUEL 30:8 ESV

Dear Father, in this scene, David had just discovered
that his family and the families of all his men had been
captured. He was distraught! As if things weren't bad
enough, the men in his camp turned on him, blaming
him for what happened. Still, David didn't act rashly. He
sought Your wisdom and Your will before taking action.
Even though he was overcome with emotion, he knew
better than to respond in haste. Too often, I act before I
pray, and the results are never good. Remind me to follow
David's example. When I'm desperate and overwhelmed,
I need to seek You first.

*Can you recall a time when you acted in
the heat of the moment instead of seeking
God's guidance? What were the results?*

A Sincere Heart

"Give your servant therefore an understanding mind to govern your people, that I may discern between good and evil, for who is able to govern this your great people?" It pleased the Lord that Solomon had asked this.

1 KINGS 3:9-10 ESV

Dear Father, You asked Solomon what he wanted. You basically gave him a blank check and told him to fill in the amount. Instead of asking for money or fame or power, he asked for Your wisdom. What a testimony to his heart! Yet Solomon wasn't perfect. He was far from it and made many mistakes in his life. I'm so glad to know You use imperfect people. Despite my flaws, I can still please You. The goal is to love You with all my heart, soul, and mind. When I love You with my whole being, I still may make mistakes. But I know You see my heart, and You're pleased with my efforts.

Have you ever worried that you're not good enough for God to use?

Filling Up Space

Finally, brothers, whatever is true, whatever is honorable, whatever is just, whatever is pure, whatever is lovely, whatever is commendable, if there is any excellence, if there is anything worthy of praise, think about these things.

PHILIPPIANS 4:8 ESV

Dear Father, these are the thoughts that should fill my mind and heart. But most days, it's a fight to push out all the bad stuff. Negative thoughts enter my brain swiftly and with ease, but it takes all my strength to drag them out. I'm learning that it's often a space issue. If I consistently fill my mind with Your Word, with gratitude for Your goodness, and with memories of Your love and Your generosity, those worries, fears, and frustrations don't have room to roost. Help me fill up, Lord—with thoughts that are true, honorable, just, pure, lovely, excellent, and praiseworthy.

What thoughts consume your mind? Take action to fill up with thoughts of God's goodness.

On Suffering

For it has been granted to you that for the sake of Christ you should not only believe in him but also suffer for his sake, engaged in the same conflict that you saw I had and now hear that I still have.

PHILIPPIANS 1:29-30 ESV

Dear Father, the idea that the Christian life is easy is a false one. Yes, You give us peace in the midst of trials, but the trials will come. You give us serenity in the storms, but the storms still happen. As a Christian, I will suffer. I will feel lost, like a foreigner in my own country. You never promised otherwise. But You did promise never to leave me or forsake me. You promised joy for the journey. And You promised that one day, at the end of this road, I'll live in a very real place, with a very real relationship with the One who created me and loves me more than anything.

How have you suffered for being a Christian?

Press On

*Not that I have already grasped it all or
have already become perfect, but I press
on if I may also take hold of that for which
I was even taken hold of by Christ Jesus.*

PHILIPPIANS 3:12 NASB

Dear Father, sometimes it's hard to keep going. Some days, it feels like everyone and everything is against me, and I don't know how I'll move forward. Thank You for this reminder that You're not finished with me. This race, this life, is worth the struggle because I know You'll be waiting at the end. You are the prize, Father! Not only will I receive my reward at the end of my life, but You pour out so many blessings along the way. I know I have a long way to go, but I will press on. Thank You for making each day worth living, each breath worth taking.

*What circumstance are you pressing
through right now? Cling to Christ,
and picture yourself as the victor.*

Words

"I tell you, on the day of judgment people will give account for every careless word they speak, for by your words you will be justified, and by your words you will be condemned."
MATTHEW 12:36-37 ESV

Dear Father, my words are important, aren't they? The book of James compares the tongue to a ship's rudder. It's a tiny instrument that holds great power. My words have the power to heal someone's hurting heart. They can also wound beyond description. Words are dangerous weapons. I would never dream of handling a fully loaded gun carelessly, slinging it around without thought for who it might harm. But I don't always take that same kind of care with the words I speak. Forgive me for the foolish things I've said, the wounds I've caused, the hearts I've hurt. Help me train myself to edit my words before I speak them. Let the things I say be a source of peace, joy, healing, and love for everyone in my path.

Are you careful with your words?

Created for Him

He is the image of the invisible God, the firstborn of all creation. For by him all things were created, in heaven and on earth, visible and invisible, whether thrones or dominions or rulers or authorities—all things were created through him and for him.
COLOSSIANS 1:15–16 ESV

Dear Father, there really is no end to Your power, is there? Your Son, Christ, is the firstborn of all creation. You have always existed, even before You created the heavens and the earth. You made everything physical that I can see and touch. You created all the forces of the spiritual world, which are every bit as real, though they're invisible to me. You fashioned everything for Yourself. As I read this, I feel ashamed that I'm so egocentric at times. I'm such a small part of the big picture, and my sole purpose is to please You. Teach me to live out that purpose with humility, understanding who I am and who You are.

What awes you most about God's creation?

Alive in Christ

*And you, who were dead in your trespasses
and the uncircumcision of your flesh, God made
alive together with him, having forgiven us all
our trespasses, by canceling the record of debt
that stood against us with its legal demands.
This he set aside, nailing it to the cross.*

COLOSSIANS 2:13–14 ESV

Dear Father, I was dead in my sin. I recall that movie from the 1990s, *Dead Man Walking*. That was me. I was physically breathing but spiritually deceased. But when I met Christ, I came alive. I don't understand how You could forgive such a great debt that I owed. You canceled it! You nailed it to the cross with a note that read "Paid in Full." I want the rest of my life to be lived as one long thank-you note. I'm so grateful, Father. Thank You for loving me that much.

*Do you feel alive in Christ? Try living in
gratitude, and feel yourself come to life.*

Focus

*If then you have been raised with Christ, seek the
things that are above, where Christ is, seated at
the right hand of God. Set your minds on things
that are above, not on things that are on earth.*
COLOSSIANS 3:1-2 ESV

Dear Father, I admit it. I get this one wrong far too often.
I want to set my mind on things above, but earthly things
clamor for my attention. And I do need to tend to those
mundane matters, Lord. I guess by "set your mind" You
mean I'm not supposed to place all my attention on those
earthly circumstances. I'm not supposed to get caught
up in them, as if they are the most important things in
my life. Even when I'm taking care of everyday business,
my focus is to remain on You and on things that please
You. Help me focus on things above. And help me point
others to Your great love.

Where is your focus?

Rejoice!

Rejoice in the Lord always; again I will say,
rejoice! Let your gentle spirit be known
to all people. The Lord is near.
PHILIPPIANS 4:4–5 NASB

Dear Father, sometimes it's easy to rejoice. Other days, not so much. Yet joy isn't a fake smile or pretending to be happy when I'm not. Joy doesn't depend on my current circumstances at all. Instead, it depends on my future. Because I'm confident in my salvation, I have joy. Because I'm confident in Your love and that You have good things in store for me, I have joy. Even in difficult circumstances, I can rejoice through those events because I know You love me, You're never far away, and You'll take care of me. Each trial provides another chance to see Your love in action. From now on, instead of getting frustrated when things don't go my way, I'll ask You to help me respond with a gentle spirit, filled with joy.

In what current circumstance can you
choose joy instead of frustration?

Absolutely Nothing

For I am sure that neither death nor life, nor angels nor rulers, nor things present nor things to come, nor powers, nor height nor depth, nor anything else in all creation, will be able to separate us from the love of God in Christ Jesus our Lord.

ROMANS 8:38–39 ESV

Dear Father, thank You for this. Just reading these words, I feel overwhelmed and grateful beyond measure. The negative voices in my head can be loud and strong, and they often leave me feeling unworthy and defeated. But how can I be unworthy if the King of kings wants me? How can I feel defeated if the Almighty God is on my side? I often feel lost and alone in this world, like I don't belong. But You promised I'll never be alone, not for a single breath. Absolutely nothing can separate me from You. These words bring such comfort, and they give me confidence, knowing I don't have to face the world alone.

Have you ever felt far away from God?

Gracious Words

Let your speech always be gracious,
seasoned with salt, so that you may know
how you ought to answer each person.
COLOSSIANS 4:6 ESV

Dear Father, these words sound nice, but they're often easier said than done. My speech isn't always gracious. It isn't always seasoned with the salt of Your wisdom. Too often, I speak in haste. If someone hurts my feelings, I try to hurt theirs. If someone makes me angry, I try to one-up them. But that kind of speech isn't fitting for a royal child of the King. Train me to hold my tongue, Father. When I start to speak from hurt or anger or pride, stop me. Interrupt me, to give me a chance to reconsider. Help me speak only words that are gracious, kind, and filled with Your love and truth.

When is the last time you spoke in haste?
Do you wish you could change that moment?

Come Quickly!

For the Lord himself will descend from heaven with a cry of command, with the voice of an archangel, and with the sound of the trumpet of God. And the dead in Christ will rise first. Then we who are alive, who are left, will be caught up together with them in the clouds to meet the Lord in the air, and so we will always be with the Lord.

1 THESSALONIANS 4:16-17 ESV

Dear Father, when I read this passage, my heart speeds up and I have to catch my breath. I'm so excited for that day! I'll be honest. . .I want You to come right now, this moment. I'm ready. The thought of leaving the problems of this world behind fills my heart with joy. But I know You're holding off because there are so many who still don't know You. Help me do my part to point them to You, every single day. Even so, I'll add this prayer: please come quickly.

Are you ready for Christ to return?

Seek to Do Good

See that no one repays anyone evil for evil,
but always seek to do good to one
another and to everyone.
1 THESSALONIANS 5:15 ESV

Dear Father, I don't consider myself an evil person. But when people hurt me or someone I love, I can turn into a bear. I've been known to stew over others' actions and consider ways I can put them in their place. That behavior may not fit the true definition of *evil*, but it's certainly not in line with this verse. I'm to seek to do good. To seek means to actively look for something. You want me to actively look for ways to show Your goodness and love to those who hurt me. Wow. That's hard. But I want to do that, Lord. Change my heart, and give me strength to repay evil and meanness with good.

Has someone hurt you recently? How can
you repay that person with good?

His Pleasure

For it was the Father's good pleasure for all the fullness to dwell in Him, and through Him to reconcile all things to Himself, whether things on earth or things in heaven, having made peace through the blood of His cross.

COLOSSIANS 1:19–20 NASB

Dear Father, I understand that You love me. That's why You sent Jesus to pay the penalty for my sins. But how can You say that was a pleasure? It must have been agonizing grief to watch Your beloved Son suffer and die. Yet, when I look at any new mother gazing on her newborn child, I see joy. I see pleasure. I see a willingness, even an eagerness, to go through all the pain of childbirth again because she loves her child that much. You look at my salvation as a pleasure because Your love for me is so great. Thank You for that kind of overwhelming love, Father.

Who do you love most in this world? God's love for you is greater than you can imagine.

Tips for Godly Living

*Rejoice always, pray without ceasing, give
thanks in all circumstances; for this is the
will of God in Christ Jesus for you.*
1 Thessalonians 5:16–18 esv

Dear Father, this passage provides a bullet-point list for behavior for those who want to lead a victorious Christian life. First, rejoice always. Really, Lord? Rejoice, even when I get a flat tire? Yet I know I can rejoice even in the midst of trials. Joy doesn't come from my circumstances, but from my future. Second, pray without ceasing. This is the easiest one for me because I love talking to You in my head, all day long. Finally, give thanks in everything. Some things are hard to be thankful for. But I can always be thankful to You for my salvation. I can be grateful that these problems are temporary. Help me, today and every day, to follow these steps to live the best life I can.

*Do you struggle to fulfill any of
Paul's suggestions in this passage?*

Love Them

The coming of the lawless one is by the activity of Satan with all power and false signs and wonders, and with all wicked deception for those who are perishing, because they refused to love the truth and so be saved.
2 Thessalonians 2:9–10 esv

Dear Father, all around me there are people who don't know You. They may seem happy on the outside, but I know You created each of us with an innate desire to know You. Satan has deceived them, and they believe they can get along just fine without You. What can I do? How can I reach them? Even as I ask those questions, I hear the answer in my head: *"Love them. Love them. Love them."* Teach me to love people as You love them, and help me point them to Your grace, goodness, and light.

Do you know someone who's been deceived by Satan? How can you love that person?

Adjusting the Schedule

For we hear that some among you walk in idleness,
not busy at work, but busybodies. Now such persons
we command and encourage in the Lord Jesus Christ
to do their work quietly and to earn their own living.
2 Thessalonians 3:11–12 esv

Dear Father, I don't want to think of myself as a busybody. Yet it's easy to get caught up in idle talk that doesn't do anything to build others up. It's easy to waste hours on social media, when I spend minutes or less each day with You. Forgive me for being idle and for spending time in activities that don't please You. Life is too short to waste on trivial things. Help me to quietly do the work You've set before me, to love others, and to shine Your light in this dark world.

How can you adjust your schedule
and actions to better please God?

Don't Grow Weary

As for you, brothers, do not grow weary in doing good.
2 THESSALONIANS 3:13 ESV

Dear Father, I'm so glad You never grow weary in doing good things for me. Even when I fail, You work tirelessly on my behalf. Even when I make poor choices, You keep loving me, caring for me, and encouraging me toward victory. Yet all too often, people make me tired. I get frustrated with their attitudes and their choices, and I just want to throw in the towel. Give me stamina when it comes to doing good for others. Make me more loving. Teach me to be an encourager. Show me ways to express kindness and compassion, mercy and grace. In other words, make me like You, Father. Give me strength and endurance to fulfill Your purpose for my life.

When have you grown weary of doing good?

Instruction Manual

All Scripture is inspired by God and beneficial for teaching, for rebuke, for correction, for training in righteousness; so that the man or woman of God may be fully capable, equipped for every good work.
2 Timothy 3:16–17 NASB

Dear Father, life has a way of throwing boulders in my path. I can't count the number of times I found myself in situations that I had no idea how to face. But You will never allow me to face anything without providing me with the wisdom and support to make it through successfully. You've provided Your Word as an instruction manual. When I try to struggle my way through without reading the instructions, I work harder, get more frustrated, and still fail. Draw me to Your Word, Father. Remind me to spend time reading life's instructions every day. As this verse says, I want to be fully capable, equipped for every good work You have planned for me to do.

Do you spend time each day reading God's Word?

Like a Lion

"He crouched, he lay down like a lion and like a lioness; who will rouse him up? Blessed are those who bless you, and cursed are those who curse you."
NUMBERS 24:9 ESV

Dear Father, the book of Revelation refers to Christ as the Lion of Judah. Sometimes when I feel anxious, I picture Him as a huge lion walking beside me, protecting me and giving me courage. I love this verse because it reminds me that I don't have to do anything but stay close to You. Like a lion with its cubs, You may give a benevolent nod to those who do me no harm, but You will fiercely protect me from those who intend evil against me. That picture in my mind gives me confidence. Thank You for Your power and protection.

What do you feel anxious about? Can you picture Christ as a lion, walking beside you?

Be Still

Moses answered the people, "Do not be afraid.
Stand firm and you will see the deliverance the
LORD will bring you today. The Egyptians you
see today you will never see again. The LORD
will fight for you; you need only to be still."
EXODUS 14:13–14 NIV

Dear Father, what a powerful reminder. So many times I feel like I must fight my battles alone. I pray, but I give You about two minutes to act before I step in front of You and take things into my own hands. It's often harder to be still than to take action. But when it comes to faith, that's what You've called me to do: Be still. Trust You. Be patient, and give You time to work. Forgive me for my stubborn, impatient will that tries to force Your hand. Teach me to trust You. Teach me to be still.

Are you facing a battle in your life? Is it
hard to be still and let God fight for you?

Fighting Temptation

The tempter came to him and said, "If you are the Son of God, tell these stones to become bread." Jesus answered, "It is written: 'Man shall not live on bread alone, but on every word that comes from the mouth of God.'"
MATTHEW 4:3-4 NIV

Dear Father, we overcome temptation with Your Word, don't we? The more of Your Word I know, the easier it is to pass through those tempting moments with victory. Your Word is a living, active thing. It's not just words on a page. Your words have power! Specifically, they have power over sin, Satan, and evil of every kind. Help me carry my sword—Your Word—like a weapon, hidden in my heart. I want it to be ready to fight at all times. Thank You for giving me everything I need to live a victorious life.

What are some temptations you face each day? Make a list of scriptures that address your situation.

He Cares

Jesus went throughout Galilee, teaching in their synagogues, proclaiming the good news of the kingdom, and healing every disease and sickness among the people. News about him spread all over Syria, and people brought to him all who were ill with various diseases, those suffering severe pain, the demon-possessed, those having seizures, and the paralyzed; and he healed them.

MATTHEW 4:23–24 NIV

Dear Father, I love how Christ met the people's practical needs as well as their spiritual needs. He didn't just try to get them "saved." It's hard to think about the spirit when your body is in pain or hungry or cold. Your care for me is complete. I can come to You with any problem I have, whether it's spiritual, emotional, mental, or physical. Thank You for taking such tender care of me. Help me to see others' needs and to do what I can to care for them as well.

What physical needs do you have right now? He cares, and He's working on your behalf.

Beyond Comprehension

"What is man, that You think of him? Or a son of man, that You are concerned about him? You have made him for a little while lower than angels; You have crowned him with glory and honor; You have put everything in subjection under his feet."

<small>HEBREWS 2:6-8 NASB</small>

Dear Father, when I think of who You are and I compare that to who I am, I feel overwhelmed. I can't understand why You think of me at all. Yet because You are love, because love drives everything You do, You've chosen me as the object of Your affection. You made me in Your image and called me Your child. You reside in my heart and give me full access to Your power, Your wisdom, Your mercy and grace. Though I don't understand it, I accept it. I want to live my life in a way that honors You and points other people to Your love.

When you think of God's love for you, what is the most difficult concept to grasp?

Blessed

"Blessed are those who hunger and thirst for righteousness, for they will be filled. Blessed are the merciful, for they will be shown mercy. Blessed are the pure in heart, for they will see God. Blessed are the peacemakers, for they will be called children of God."

MATTHEW 5:6–9 NIV

Dear Father, Your Word contains so many promises. These are only a few of them. You promise, over and over, that when we pattern our lives after Your character, You will bless us. When I long to be righteous, You will make it so. When I respond to others with mercy, You'll show mercy to me. When I love You with a pure, all-consuming love, I will see Your presence in every facet of my life. And when I do my best to create peace in the midst of chaos, You claim me as Your own child. Each of these qualities is a reflection of Yourself. Make me like You, Father.

Which of these qualities comes easiest for you? Which is the hardest?

Incomprehensible

"Holy, holy, holy, is the Lord God Almighty,
who was and is and is to come!"

REVELATION 4:8 ESV

Dear Father, I want to say this verse, these words, again and again. I want their truth to sink through my skin, deep into my spirit. You are holy! You are perfect, without flaw. The idea that You, the Holy God, would want a relationship with me is incomprehensible. The fact that You are eternal, immortal, and almighty and yet You can be known by someone like me is beyond my understanding. Your love is beautiful beyond words. Your presence in my life is inconceivable. But I'm so grateful, Father, that You choose to love me. You love me because You are love, and that love overwhelms me. I have nothing to offer You but myself. Today and every day, I am Yours. Do with me as You will.

How has God's love changed you?

Topical Index

About the Author

Renae Brumbaugh Green lives in Texas with her handsome, country-boy husband, two dogs, a bunch of chickens, and a duck. She teaches English and writing at Tarleton State University, writes a column for several newspapers, and writes books for children and grown-ups. In her free time, she does fun things with her four grown children, forces herself to exercise, reads historical fiction, and takes naps.

GOT 3 MINUTES?

3-Minute Prayers for the Worried Heart

This devotional prayer book packs a powerful dose of inspiration into just-right-sized readings to you live a stress-free life. Each prayer, written specifically for devotional quiet time, is complemented by a relevant scripture and question for further thought.

Paperback / 978-1-63609-415-1

3-Minute Devotions for Hope and Healing

This delightful devotional packs a powerful dose of encouragement, hope, and healing into 180 just-right-sized readings for you. Minute 1: scripture to meditate on; Minute 2: a short devotional reading; Minute 3: a prayer. Each day's reading is the ideal way for you to begin or end your day.

Paperback / 978-1-63609-352-9

Find these and More from Barbour Publishing at Your Favorite Bookstore or at www.barbourbooks.com

BARBOUR
PUBLISHING